THE BLUE LADY

A Tale of a Ship

THE BLUE LADY

A Tale of a Ship

SANJAY PARIKH

YATRA
An imprint of Vani Prakashan Group

vaniprakashan.com

Hardback First Edition : 2025

Yatra Books is an imprint of Vani Prakashan Group

Head Office

4695, 21-A, Daryaganj, New Delhi-110 002, India
Phone : +91 11 23273167, 23275710

Registered Bookstores and Offices

Ashok Rajpath, Patna-800 004, Bihar
Coffee House Campus, Mahatma Gandhi Marg, Prayagraj-211 001, Uttar Pradesh
Mahatma Gandhi Antarrashtriya Hindi Vishwavidyalaya, Wardha-442 001, Maharashtra
sales@vaniprakashan.in
vaniprakashan@gmail.com

The Blue Lady : A Tale of a Ship
by Sanjay Parikh

ISBN : 978-93-48235-11-4
History

Price : ₹ 499

Printed and bound in India at City Press, Delhi-110095

In fond memory of my younger brother
Madhu Sudan
who left behind the fragrance of goodness
and human values.

Acknowledgement

The idea of the book was conceived long back. However, the narration and style kept changing. Besides legal preoccupation, many worldly distractions also delayed the book. When I narrated my idea about the book, Ritwick Dutta showed keen interest. That was the beginning. Prachi Arya and Maneka Kaur assisted me in collecting relevant material and collating important information. Their research helped me immensely. I wish to thank both of them for their support and encouragement. I also took help from Satwik Parikh, Maulshree Pathak, Dr. Shikhar Ranjan and Gopal Krishna. I greatly value their assistance. My wife Vandana Parikh went through the draft and suggested a few corrections – many thanks to her. Kritika finally looked at the draft minutely which was very helpful. I express my sincere thanks to her. I am also grateful to Aditi Maheshwari of Vani Prakashan, who liked the theme of this book and readily agreed to publish it. Not only this, but she also gave a few constructive ideas.

True to his nature, Claude Alvares initially expressed doubts about the theme, but upon reading the draft, his encouragement spurred me on to completion. He and Norma Alvares generously dedicated their precious time to editing the book, a gesture I will never forget. Their caring, sensitive, and affectionate nature, so rare in today's world, has been a source of strength throughout this process.

I acknowledge all those who played some part, however small, in completing this book. Their collective efforts have made this book a reality. I am genuinely grateful to each one of them.

—Sanjay Parikh

Preface

It is not usual to find a senior counsel actively practising in the Supreme Court of India finding the time to write a book of this kind—with ingredients that are part history, part law and part romance. But Sanjay Parikh has always been a different species of lawyer. Determined to ensure that he does not expend and exhaust his entire life in the one-dimensional pursuit of pleading other people's worthy causes in court, he has zealously carved time out from lawyering for other less cantankerous and even soul-enhancing pursuits. These include poetry, painting, occasional wood carving, and, believe it or not, organic farming. In fact, Parikh is unique in being one of few lawyers with several volumes of Hindi poetry to his credit.

His involvement in such "extra-legal affairs" has had its own benign and beneficial impact on the quality, sincerity and depth of his pleading in court rooms and out. He has expanded specific legal cases onto a larger-than-life canvas. His decade-long work as a lawyer through the National Human Rights Commission to prevent further tribal starvation deaths for which Kalahandi in Odisha became a household name ended up as a successful book, *The Courts and Hunger.* Naturally, this has incited him to turn another of his persisting Supreme Court cases into the present book, which deals with human obsessions with grand, much-celebrated, ocean-going ships (including passenger liners and cruise vessels) and their ultimate ignominious exit at the world's biggest graveyard for condemned ships, located at Alang in Gujarat.

Parikh's encounter with Europe's grand ships and the problems they faced with the Indian judiciary first started when he got involved with the writ petition filed before the Supreme Court by Dr Vandana Shiva's Research Foundation for Science, Technology and Ecology (RFSTE) in 1995. The petition challenged India's casual imports of hazardous wastes–which included waste oil, zinc waste, lead-acid batteries, and sometimes even garbage–from industrialized countries.

The petitioner argued that the import of such hazardous wastes into the country was contrary to agreements made by the world community under the Basel Convention on the Transboundary Movement of Hazardous Wastes. For several years prior to the filing of the petition–and despite the Convention coming into force–large quantities of hazardous wastes continued to land on India's shores. Ostensibly, this was for the country's recycling industry. India is famous for recycling. We recycle everything. Our house makers recycle cans, bottles and jars. We import waste paper thrown out by municipalities of developed nations and turn it into useful products. We import used edible oil since European regulations do not permit its reuse, but ours do. A few months after the 9/11 demolition of the Twin Towers in New York took place, the debris of both towers ended up at Chennai port. This was, to say the least, quite scandalous. No sane-thinking Indian, who is convinced that India should not be treated as a dumping ground for other countries' unwanted, problematic and undesirable wastes, would accept it. In fact, it became quite clear that in addition to honest recycling, substantial wastes were being imported by unscrupulous traders simply for dumping in the Indian subcontinent. The primary objective of the Basel Convention itself had been to prohibit precisely such illegal dumping activity by developed countries in poor or developing countries.

Sanjay Parikh represented this important cause before the Supreme Court, which took more than a decade. He argued the case *pro bono* because it disturbed him also as an environmentalist and human rights activist. If the Court responded, it was simply because it found it had standing before it an extremely diligent, well-researched counsel conversant with every aspect of the legal handling of hazardous wastes. On one such occasion, we were able to witness Mr. Parikh, over a period of 15 days, patiently reading and explaining the report of the M.G.K. Menon Committee on the subject to the bench to whom the case was assigned. He was "on legs" every day for those two weeks from 11 in the morning till the court rose for the day. Sometimes he would call us for clarification. We readily obliged as these issues bothered us as well.

The court, in 1997, had set up the M.G.K. Menon High Powered Committee on the Management of Hazardous Wastes to advise it on the measures needed to deal with the issues involved in the import of such wastes, considering their overall complexity. The Court had also asked the HPC (as it came to be known) to look at domestically generated hazardous wastes and how they were being handled. The HPC worked from 1997 till 2000 and submitted a detailed report to the apex court highlighting its findings, flagging important chronic issues and making several recommendations, most of which the Court accepted.

One major problem the HPC noticed was the issue of old or condemned ships being brought to Indian shores for dismantling. As mentioned earlier, India hosts the world's largest graveyard for condemned ships at Alang. Conventionally, at least in industrialized countries, old ships are dismantled in docks and broken with huge reliance on technology and stricter environmental norms. At Alang, ships were not dismantled in docks. Instead, those who purchase the vessel for scrap simply use the natural advantage of Alang's beach slope and the huge difference between low and high tide on that coast to run the ship directly onto the beach ("beaching"). Once secured to the beach, the condemned ship is taken down piece by piece through the astonishing skills of hundreds of specialized workers using elementary equipment and their bare hands. Not only did people die in this extremely hazardous operation, but the natural environment got damaged as well, as toxic elements from these ships were set loose in the natural environment. The dismantling process generated heavy metals like lead, mercury, cadmium, and other metals, including iron, alloys, aluminium, and zinc. Much of that, together with waste oil, went into the sea.

The other problem with the ship-breaking industry–and the reason why it became entangled in the hazardous waste issue–was that many of the ships having been constructed several decades ago contained substances that are now routinely considered hazardous and would therefore, on the ship's dismantling, become hazardous wastes. These included mainly large volumes of asbestos, but also PCBs (polychlorinated biphenyls–carcinogenic chemical compounds, banned now in the West), spent oil, and sometimes, even radioactive components. Who was responsible for ensuring the environmentally friendly disposal of such wastes generated during the recovery of the useful materials from the ship? The exporting country or the importer? Where were the owners of the Alang ship-breaking yards dumping these wastes? That's where the HPC came in.

Two of its members (Dr V.K. Iya–a BARC scientist, and one of us) were deputed to visit Alang and to submit a report. In fact, we visited Alang with the clear conviction that it should be permanently shut down, having seen umpteen reports, many international ones, on the serious violations of safe working conditions, leading to deaths and injuries, in addition to the serious damage the ship breaking activities were having on the natural environment, including the generation of huge volumes of hazardous wastes–all problems sourced to a completely unregulated industry.

What changed our minds on our very first visit there was the 6-8 km road drive before we reached Alang itself. We were simply taken aback at what we saw. All along the road, on both sides, and for its entire length, we encountered countless stalls with merchandize salvaged from the dismantled ships. Unaware, we were, in fact, passing through one of the "re-cycling hotspots" of the planet. Every part of the ships broken down at Alang including their crockery, furniture, upholstery, bathroom fittings, microwave ovens, washing machines, coolers and air conditioners, engines, etc., had been carefully removed, intact, in its working condition, and put on display and sale at the stalls. We were told that the shops were visited by newly-wed couples to stock their new homes with good quality imported materials. Also on sale for factory owners were heavy-duty generator sets, welding equipment, turbochargers, air purifiers and whatnot. (Many ships had original art pieces strung up in ballrooms, dining areas and exclusive cabins. However, these were auctioned off to discerning customers before they left for India)

But besides the above, the steel plates from the massive body of the broken-down ship went to factories and comprised between 10-15% of the production from India's steel rolling mills. (In 2021, for example, Alang's yards added some 3.5 million tonnes of steel to India's production of the commodity. (That has generally been the average annual production of recycled metal from this source.) The world is conversant with the havoc that iron ore mining has caused to the planet's ecology and environment. The more metal we recycle, the less we need to extract from the bowels of the earth. So, there was simply no way a committee of experts who were also environmentalists would have shut down a recycling operation of this scale. The option was to ensure the activity met the standards laid down by the hazardous waste rules and various Supreme Court orders.

The vessels that came to be broken up at Alang were the crème-de-la-crème of the shipping world. They all had prestigious names: the *Scandinavian Star,* the *Sea Giant*, the *SS Albatross*, the *SS Magellan*, and the *SS Columbus*. The list is quite endless. During their active lives, these ships rode the waves with great majesty to the utter awe of their passengers. People visited ports and harbours just to have a look at them when they berthed, stunned at the sheer audacity of their size. Some of these liners were exclusive bastions of privilege, but most criss-crossed the oceans with hundreds of passengers and goods–before the entry of cruise liners enabled people to wallow aimlessly from port to port and back again home under the guise of a vacation.

During their construction and during their heyday, nobody even dreamed that the dismantling of these giants, when finally decided by their owners, would get ensnared in the various provisions of the Basel Convention or the Indian hazardous waste rules. The issue of whether such ships themselves ought to be considered hazardous waste (because of the hazardous materials used in their construction and embedded in their bodies) and, later, whether they should be de-toxified prior to arrival at the Alang ship breaking yard became a serious contentious and contested issue that would occupy several days across several years of the apex court's valuable time from the period 2003 to 2020. In fact, some issues still remain unsolved!

Parikh's book, if it had been conventionally written, would have been, at the most, a fairly faithful volume on the ways in which rich countries dump their wastes, including their old ships, on poor countries, with a discussion on attendant conventions, legal provisions and judicial orders. This would have interested, at the most, a fraction of the legal fraternity. So, he did the next best thing: he turned his narrative into a romantic autobiography of one of the grandest ships ever to cross the oceans, christened at birth as the *SS France*–a grand symbol and display of French national pride–rechristened shortly before her death as *The Blue Lady*. In order to add some spice to his tale, he peppered the narrative with some fairly entrancing stories of the very famous people who boarded the *SS France*. These included Salvador Dali–the world-renowned surrealist painter–famous film actors including Cary Grant and Audrey Hepburn, and others equally celebrated including the Beatles and authors like Tennessee Williams. *The Blue Lady* narrates a gripping account of the high-security transport within her holds of da Vinci's *Mona Lisa* from the Louvre in Paris, France, to the USA. The loan of the painting by the French government to enable thousands of Americans to view it on US soil was made possible through the sheer charm and persuasive skills of Ms Jacqueline Kennedy (later, Onassis).

Parikh deftly interweaves the account of *The Blue Lady's* origins and domination of the ocean waves with stories of the other grand ships that either preceded her, would attempt to rival her, or would succeed her. The book narrates stories of the birth, life and times of a number of other elegant dames of the sea, including the *SS Normandie*, the *SS Liberte'*, the *SS Clemenceau*, the *SS Europa* and the *RMS Queen Elizabeth*. Parikh does this through a creative but wholly imagined distillate of the endless, mostly trivial, gossip that presumably gripped the voyagers on these boats, captive as they were to gratuitous awards of copious amounts of time and leisure, delinked from the world of work and daily preoccupations, and literally prisoners of the ocean's waters between the long periods that the ship left one port and before it could sail into another.

In the second part of the book, Parikh deals with how these imposing vessels, towards the end of their extravagant lives, got mired in legal battles that simply refused to go away.

As members of the HPC first and later of the Supreme Court Monitoring Committee (SCMC), we found we had more than our hands filled with them. Though we boarded them at Alang, we hardly ever got the opportunity to sail in any of them! The ship-breaking issue migrated across several benches of the Supreme Court, and this voyage through too many legal oceans may have precipitated the steady deterioration of the manner in which the Apex Court finally dealt with the controversies posed by their dismantling. Sanjay Parikh is harsh, and with good reason, in his assessment of the apex court's later orders that made it possible for The *Blue Lady* to be beached at Alang. Its owners forced the beaching of the ship almost in defiance, and the apex court tamely accepted the *fait accompli*.

What did the judicial adjudication eventually achieve in terms of its handling of ship breaking as a hazardous waste? Did we move forward or backwards? Has the working environment improved at Alang (now expanded to Sosiya further north of Alang) for both people and nature?

As far as the ship breaking industry is concerned, in order to fill an obvious vacuum–and partly to mitigate international criticism of Alang ship-breaking practices–Parliament passed the Recycling of Ships Bill. It became an Act after it received the assent of the President of India on 13th December 2019. The new Act now provides for the regulated breaking of ships. The Act is compliant with the provisions of the Hong Kong International Convention for the Safe and Environmentally Sound Recycling of Ships, 2009, endorsed by the International Marine Organization.

But the Supreme Court's scrutiny of Alang also led to the steady improvement of housekeeping and work practices at that location. However, workers still die at Alang, explosions still occur, and injuries get recorded despite the fact that the yards are now under a stricter regime than earlier.

About the discarded asbestos waste–also found in *The Blue Lady*–and PCBs, we still have no idea of the quantities extracted or isolated and whether and where they have been safely disposed of. We do not have any study on the cumulative impact of all those heavy metals and other toxins that have entered the Alang sea over the past 30 years. The position of the disposal of toxic waste generated now at Alang is also not clear. Despite this, the Gujarat government has prepared a master plan to increase the number of plots (last count, there were something between 150-180 yards) by adding another 50 to the existing ones.

Sanjay Parikh's *Blue Lady* may not tell of every one of these issues. It is worth a read nonetheless, not just by all those who love cruise vessels and passenger liners (the last already in severe decline with the advent of affordable air travel), but by non-legal professionals and the public as well. In the end, the story of the *Blue Lady* is also a story of us all, of hubris–the illness that severely affects all human beings, which would now appear from Parikh's tale, affects these imposing floating palaces as well. For all the fame and name, the adoration and the awe, the grand entries and exits, the days of ill-fame, sorrow and dismantling must always arrive. In our case, however, we are not banished from our loved spaces, the countries of our birth, when we die. But in the case of these giant ships, the internment is almost always abandonment on a faraway foreign shore, forsaken by one's own proud country and adoring crowds, turned into an item of unseemly haggling between scrap dealers and to top the humiliation, treated little more than a mountain of hazardous wastes, to be cut, extracted, melted, junked or sold. What a travesty of an ending, indeed!

Well, what about the general situation of hazardous waste handling within the country and illegal imports? Did *that* improve? Whether this long litigation brought some change? For one thing, we got enhanced regulation. The Hazardous Waste Rules 1987 were amended to further align with the Basel Convention. All over the country, Hazardous Waste Treatment and Disposal Facilities (TSDFs) were set up with the central government's support to receive hazardous wastes from Indian industrial units. All such units were only able to operate under an authorization issued by the state's Pollution Control Board. By 2007, a total of Rs.2500 crores had been spent by all actors to clean up hazardous waste dumping sites and set up TSDFs. Hundreds of barrels of imported waste oil lying unclaimed at ports were sent to TSDFs for incineration under direct orders of the apex court. But still, dumps of hazardous waste lying in different states, which were identified by the Supreme Court Monitoring Committee, are lying untreated, and fire accidents take place in the TSDFs due to unsafe handling.

Today we ought to be wiser. We know that more regulations and laws simply do not eliminate such problems. They may help mitigate a difficult situation somewhat but do not provide permanent solutions. Matters cannot drastically improve unless industry is willing to concede that it does not have an inalienable right to generate hazardous wastes; till Western countries are compelled to admit they cannot get rid of their wastes by dumping them in other parts of the planet. One of the most interesting changes in India's hazardous waste rules is the requirement that every industrial unit, when it comes to renewal of its permit, must provide proof of efforts it has made since the last permit issued to it to reduce its generation of such wastes through use of better technology. If Pollution Control Boards enforce this regulation, much will change for the better and Parikh's enormous extraordinary contribution in dealing with these issues before the Supreme Court of India is not mindlessly squandered, or in the language of the ship breakers, "beached."

But beyond law is the emotional fervour that grips the tale throughout the *Blue Lady's* inimitable narration. At times we become one with her tribulations. That is the author's biggest achievement!

Dr. Claude Alvares
Dr. Dilip B Boralkar

Introduction

Everything that exists on this earth, from the smallest to the biggest, has a story to tell. Footprints of its life remain forever etched in the memories of the time. It is for the storyteller to weave the shades and shines, joys and sorrows, despair and happiness, love and dejection in a manner that brings the narrative to life.

But this is a tale that weaves within itself a narrative, a course of events, several stories, where someone speaks, and others listen. It fills in the blanks with the help of the imagination without distorting the facts. These imaginations more or less proceed on predictable lines. In a given time and space, if the events are known, one can say with confidence how things must have proceeded, how people would have reacted and what they would have said!

Craving for adventure and hunting for hidden treasures have always remained a human curiosity; only their outer form has changed with time. The call of the unknown has led humans to walk on mountainous terrains, to witness their snow-covered peaks and their beautiful mornings and sunsets. The deserts have lured them to see how a mirage creates illusions in the mind, yet the urge has nonetheless driven them to walk under the scorching sun and boiling sands. Similar desires have driven them to explore the vastness of the sea and its unending waves.

Thus began the sea voyages–initially on the bunch of logs tied together–later followed by boats and then ships. These voyages, which commenced at the beginning of civilisation, were for fishing, trade or for discovering new places. Whether they used boats or ships, they were simply arduous and unsafe.

By 1400, sea voyages had become quite prominent. The era, in fact, is known as the "Age of Exploration". In 1498, a Portuguese traveller, Vasco da Gama, discovered the sea route to India. Gradually, these ships grew more gigantic and magnificent in size. The sea journey naturally became safer and more comfortable. Passenger liners had started as early as 1840.

We all know about the *Titanic*–which had all possible physical comforts and could carry more than 1500 passengers, including the crew–and its tragic end in 1912.

The *SS France*–France's national pride–was launched as the country's showpiece in 1960, following in the tradition of one of the most elegant and beautiful passenger liners of the time–the *SS Normandie*–also known as the 'Ship of Lights.'

The *SS France* made many remarkable voyages. As times changed, she went through changes as well. From a passenger liner, she metamorphosed into the *SS Norway*, a cruise liner, and at the end of her days, condemned as scrap, she acquired the name of the *Blue Lady*.

The *Blue Lady* is, therefore, the tale of a majestic passenger liner, its glory and grandeur and the trials and tribulations she faced while laying herself bare before the vast ocean. While history contains the names of great and royal passengers she carried, her heart withheld many secrets, intrigues, deceits and conspiracies. She watched time moving. Once, the Mona Lisa–one of the world's greatest works of art–chose to travel with her from France to New York. So did Salvador Dali, the great surrealist painter, and many other famous writers and celebrities.

For the *Blue Lady*, every journey was a different experience: exploring the endless, open blue sky, the limitless ocean and the people aboard. She must have thought in those moments that she was invincible and that her charm and glory would never fade. But time was moving on. Whatever is created is bound to perish one day. The *Blue Lady* would also meet her final destiny. Her final years were turned into a saga of insults, falsehoods, betrayal, long legal battles and disappointments. What the *Blue Lady*–once the pride of France–experienced as she neared her end was certainly not the treatment she deserved!

So here is the tale narrated by the *Blue Lady* herself, in her inimitable style, based upon what she saw, observed, overheard and experienced during her long sea voyages. She speaks about *Normandie* and *Liberte'*, two other well-known passenger liners of the time. She also narrates the story of the mighty warship, the *SS Clemenceau*. We do not know whether during their long journeys, the *Blue Lady* and the *Clemenceau* ever met though they were contemporaries. The *Clemenceau* once carried a huge army and fought many battles during the Second World War. Wherever she went, she left behind a trail of terror and devastation. She also imagined the war would never end and that her dominance would last forever.

But the war had to end one day. The *Clemenceau* then discovered the vainness of her power. She too faced neglect and humiliation. Eventually she was shunned by the very country she fought for. Nobody was willing to take her during her final days. At one point, she travelled a long distance to reach India in order to embrace her ultimate end. But it was not to be her fate. She was recalled to France, from where she was taken to a British shipyard for dismantling. She met her end there.

In the first part, this book contains besides the wonderful memories and experiences of the *Blue Lady*, the tales of these glorious ships and their eventual downfall.

The second part narrates the legal battle fought in the Supreme Court of India over the *Blue Lady*. The facts prove that real justice is always elusive. The idea of justice changes with the perceptions of individual judges, their learning, upbringing, sensitivities, insensitivities and the baggage they carry within themselves. Subjective biases enter and disrupt clear thinking if the mind is not cultivated consciously with objectivity tempered by knowledge. A good judge will always be aware of the limitations of the mind and will keep trying to achieve the pinnacles of justice. It happens many a time that some orders of the court written after comprehending the problem in its totality and after understanding all related dimensions, are diluted by subsequent orders. In so doing, the obvious is often glossed over. This book touches on some of these aspects as well. Though the tale is in the nature of a monologue, the facts, which include the legal narratives, are based on events and available documents; some of them being annexed at the end of the book.

The idea of this book and its writing actually started a while ago, but the exercise was delayed due to my engagements and commitments. After every break–which at times was long–I had to redo the exercise of looking again into every detail to the extent possible. The book was written in segments that were later tied up together. There were several rounds of revisions and reformulations.

Nevertheless, I feel that time has not affected the relevance of these issues. The *Titanic* continues to be in the news even after 100 years of its sinking. Recently, in June 2023, five persons who had gone underwater to explore its wreckage, unfortunately died. But I know these tragedies will not deter people from exploring the mysteries that continue to hover around that majestic ship. Like the *Titanic*, the *Blue Lady* also continues to be in the news. People do not want to forget these historic ships; their memories are like an endless saga.

The *Blue Lady* case in the Supreme Court also illuminates how international law can influence domestic perceptions, and bring a change in the national law. Incorporating the Basel Convention as a part of 'life' under Art. 21 of the Indian Constitution became an important development in International law. The Indian Supreme Court ruled that the Basel Convention led to the enhancement of the content of 'life and environment' and therefore, it would be treated as a part of life. The Basel Convention judgment of the Supreme Court (2013) became the subject of discussion among the experts of international law. Many important journals carried articles on its international ramifications.

For each chapter, the sources of facts relied upon have been provided in the references. I acknowledge them. Similarly, the source of images has also been mentioned in the references. That too I similarly acknowledge. The facts as they exist have been weaved through imagination, as already stated above to suit the tale which *Blue Lady* would have narrated had she been alive!

I have not provided foot-notes. Instead, I have chosen to provide references at the end because foot-notes were not going along with the tale; they seemed to distract from the narrative. Instead, I have added 'Notes' for the convenience of readers to understand certain expressions and events. The sources of those notes have been mentioned therein. Notes on legal aspects are from the legal documents. The title of the present book was inspired by one of Jonathan Swift's satires–'A Tale of a Tub'.

My advantage in writing this book was that I was not only a counsel who argued the case against the dumping of hazardous wastes in India but also attempted to give this legal battle a larger dimension, i.e., fighting against the dumping of toxic wastes by the OECD countries in India who assumed to assert their dominance that India was an undeveloped country, suffering from poverty and dearth of legal regulations and therefore, such dumping was permissible. This was a sort of insult and indignity not only to India – a sovereign country–but also to its people. The litigation also exposed the true face of the developed countries on the global level, and how environmental issues and human concerns are perceived and implemented in self-interest by nations.

I hope you will enjoy reading *A Tale of a Ship* and draw parallels from it for your own journey across the sea of life!

—Sanjay Parikh

Contents

PART-IV: The Story of *SS Clemenceau*

PART-V: My Final Days

PART-I

Beginnings

Blue Lady is my name

My name is *Blue Lady.*

Does that sound intriguing? Does it evoke an image of a charming lady dressed in blue, enveloped in an air of enigma?

"Who is she?" you might wonder.

No. I am not a young lady of superior beauty and charm. I am a ship. To be precise–a passenger liner. It is true that I once carried a certain feminine beauty and elegance. In fact, I dominated the vast blue ocean as a darling of everyone for several years. Crowds would invariably be awaiting my arrival at the port just to get a glimpse of me. So, yes, I am not a beautiful lady but do listen to my story. I assure you that you will not be disappointed. You are free to form your own opinion, of course, and maybe disagree with me or simply sympathise with what I have to tell.

Though I am proud of myself and the past that I carry, at this juncture, I confess that I feel utterly lonely. I want to talk to someone. Even while I am telling you my story, I am on the verge of death in an alien land – at Alang, a known ship-breaking yard, located in Gujarat, on the west coast of India.

Blue Lady was not my name, to begin with. It was given to me almost overnight when my days of glory were over and I had nothing significant left of me to attract anybody, let alone the world. These are strange coincidences. How did I come to be here at Alang after being once hailed as the pride of France? Who brought me here? What did I see during my voyages? Who all travelled with me? I wish to tell you everything in my own words – like a tale – before I meet my end. I may sound a little eccentric at times and occasionally appear to be wanting to show off my knowledge of people and things. But once you consider my predicament, I do not doubt that you will forgive me.

As a ship, I travelled vast distances and met large number of people. Some people were, by nature, quite friendly, so I also liked them. But some turned out to be very rude, often for no rhyme or reason. I experienced the coldest of insensitivities – some dark and brutal – and shudder with fear at those memories. Could anyone be so inhuman? I witnessed love, hatred, jealousy and greed. I also saw how suddenly love turns into hate and greed destroys human compassion. These events shocked as well as surprised me. But it was futile to keep notes of all the details. At times, things became so unpredictable and so uncertain that I finally decided I would not get involved in them any longer and instead be simply an observer. But let me be honest, when you observe, you get involved, whether you are aware or not.

Many wonderful people travelled with me. Some, indeed, had beautiful hearts–overflowing with love and compassion and with transparent faces. At the same time, I also hosted royal couples who always came to display their wealth and attitude. Even that was interesting for a while. But I soon got bored of the shallowness. Then, there were also those who appeared to be searching for something in the loneliness of the vast ocean. There were poets, writers, and artists who painted their thoughts in words and colours. They always had a serious air about them. Strangely, despite what they knew, they would end up comparing: who among them was superior–the poet, the writer or the artist? Comparative charts would be drawn up with yardsticks of their self-righteous views but never reaching any conclusion. After an interval, the same sickening exercise would commence all over again. I think the human mind is like that. Some constant preoccupation is required to keep it alive. But what amazed me was that after days spent discussing serious matters relating to art and literature, things would invariably degenerate to the level of worldly gossip. And then the atmosphere of comparisons, jealousies and hatred would loom even larger than the ocean. It would appear as if whatever they discussed so seriously over all those days was only with the intent to kill time. Human beings, I wonder, have yet to learn the art of how to live Time!

But this is all just blabber! I must return to my story. Should I tell it to you chronologically, with a list of dates and events, as happens in courts? That would be quite boring. Chronology, of course, brings in discipline, but it also kills creativity unless it is self-imposed and for a purpose. I am not writing an autobiography–there is no time left for that now. In any case, most autobiographies are dull. Oh! You want to differ? I find there are too many 'I's' in them. Even when the writer wants to appear modest and humble (superficially!), the ego creeps in surreptitiously.

And please tell me, who is interested in knowing when you slept, what you read, what you achieved and what you saw in your dreams except when it is to compare with what others have done? How does one write so much about oneself? Probably the human desire is to be immortal: that people remember you, your problems and the hard work you did to overcome every difficulty you faced in life. How, from a humble beginning, you achieved a position of note in society–with wealth, name, power, etc., etc. Somehow, I am unable to do that. I would rather break from discipline and go random. I will, of course, tell you stories–real, not imaginary–except where some embellishment is necessary in order to fill the gaps. I have no doubt you will enjoy them!

Though I am at the end of my long journey, I am not filled with sadness. Perhaps silence has taught me the virtues of self-observation. In any case, when you are awaiting death, memories vividly arise before your eyes–of your birth, childhood, youth and its gradual decline. I can see everything clearly. Please listen to me carefully, I humbly insist!

Throughout my voyages, I had no idle time during the day as it was always fully packed. There was so much to see all around: people watching people, playing games or sitting idly by, chatting, laughing, dozing off in the sun or silently looking out at the vast sea. Some passengers were sick habitually and others due to the sea! Day time would always be great fun–there was never a dull moment. It was like watching a drama with varied characters and themes–amusing and hilarious. I am sure you must have enjoyed watching people while sitting in some corner. It is so relaxing, besides great learning!

Only during the night did I feel alone–in the unfathomable silence and darkness pervading all around, which at times hummed as if in contemplation, but mostly the sea's ferocious waves would hiss with anger. I would then ponder the day's affairs, choose from them what I should keep in memory and what I should throw into the surging waves so they did not return.

To tell you the truth, it is this discipline which kept me sane all these years. Probably something everyone should do! However, discarding useless accumulations from the mind is easier said than done. You need to observe constantly and unburden the self regularly! Let me be candid, I was never tempted to peep inside people's rooms at night to pry into their private lives–perhaps because enough was on display during the day. Pardon me, you may be right, instead of concentrating on telling my story, if I diverge to write about those incidents, I would be considered an accomplished gossip monger. Maybe, I would even be entitled to an award as the world's best gossip monger!

So where do I begin?

I choose the story of a young man who is still uppermost in my mind. He must have been in his late twenties. He had a fair complexion, long hair and dreamy eyes. Every night, while I was alone pondering over the day's events, he would emerge on the deck. Then, he would stand there for hours looking at the sea. He appeared to be quite fearless as I often saw him standing against the immediate backdrop of rising waves and high tides. But what was he searching for? Initially, I imagined he might be waiting for his girlfriend, like any other young man. But that thought appeared inappropriate after a few days. One day, I witnessed a security man quarrelling with him over his safety.

The young man, however, was quite well-behaved and responded very softly. I had heard his voice for the first time; it was extremely pleasant. Their conversation continued for some time. Suddenly I found both of them laughing hilariously. I was curious to know what interesting dialogue had transpired between the two of them, but of course, nothing was audible against the roar and noise of the sea. I was happy to note that from that day onwards, the security man did not stop him from coming there. My happiness was not for unknown reasons: first, he was not a disturbance in my musings; his presence had a soothing touch and second—and this I must admit—I could not wait for him to emerge, night after night!

Had I fallen in love with him? Not in the least. It had probably become a routine, a habit. I know it is difficult to distinguish between habit and infatuation, but my experiences have taught me when the sea would remain silent and when the turbulence would return. That was enough to know the mind. One evening, the young man arrived on deck with a violin! He seemed to be quite adept at playing the instrument. His first notes were so enchanting, that he held my rapt attention throughout. It was indeed a treat for the ears. He played the violin for over an hour. He also sang in between. The music was so mellifluous that I felt like asking him to play continuously–uninterrupted. But then he packed up to go back to his room. It was sometime after midnight. When he turned, I saw that there were tears in his eyes.

The next morning, as we had reached New York, he disembarked. I thought he would turn back, at least once, so that I could look at him for the last time, but he walked away at a slow pace, unlike the other passengers who were running and jostling with each other–joyous at arriving back home after months of sea voyage. I kept remembering him for months. His face appeared many a time in the silences of the long nights. Though his memory no longer haunts me now, he remains still for me a man of mystery – alone and detached. But why were there tears in his eyes that day? Perhaps I will never know.

My birth

I was proposed to be born as a passenger liner of elegance, to match my predecessors. So, a considerable debate took place regarding how I could be built, not only to look more magnificent and superior but to move faster as well. After all, I was going to be the latest in the *genre* of grand French ocean liners. In my family of such ocean liners, the traditions had already been set by the *SS Normandie* and the *SS Liberte'*. Charles De Gaulle[1]–who later became the President of France–in fact, wanted me to be a 'showcase' for France–an expression of national pride! I was expected to fulfil all these grand ambitions. But how could anyone's future be burdened with so many expectations? You must be aware of how innocent children are crushed–even before birth–by

Launch of *SS France*

the long list of ambitions their parents already carry with them. During my journeys, I witnessed parents constantly instructing their children on how they should conduct themselves, what they should read, and above all what they should aspire to become: a doctor, an engineer or a lawyer. It was quite amusing to see the response on their faces. One child said he wanted to be a steward, presumably because all the ship's stewards were smartly dressed! In one such instance, I remember a child saying he did not want to be "anybody", but his parents kept on explaining to him for many days the importance of becoming "somebody"!! How stupid of them. But that is precisely the reason why the world is so full of mediocre people.

I apologize, as these ruminations have nothing really to do with the story of my birth and I am sure there is nothing seriously wrong in the desire to stoke national pride. It could just be that I have probably turned senile–too many journeys, too many monologues and above all, the situation I am facing today. From every small thing, I start weaving some images. This happens when you have seen too much in your life, but the time to recount all that is very little.

So, back to my story.

I was relating to you that I had been chosen to be the nation's pride, but not all agreed with this idea! While some insisted that a project involving the creation of an ocean liner should be publicly funded, others questioned the need to spend so much money on a ship. So there was a heated debate on this issue in the French Parliament which lasted for three and a half years! Can you believe this? A great debate indeed on nation-building! I figure that it would have been easier to build the grand ship on time and save public money spent in these long debates. You may be right that having some debate is still better than just raising hands in support of a motion without knowing anything about the subject! If anyone raised a question, the answer was ready: 'Hey dear, you know, it's for a great cause!' Democracy has its own virtues and shortfalls!

The good news was that the letter commissioning the project was finally signed by the Chairman of the Compagnie Generale Transatlantique[2] on 25th July, 1956. Further discussions thereafter on the form, design and cost of construction consumed another year. The process of actual construction–with huge steel plates and fabrication work–continued for another four years. The hull (labelled, Hull G-19) was specially fabricated by the Chantiers de l'Atlantique Shipyard, Saint-Nazaire[3], France. With a length of 1035 feet, I was already the longest ocean liner at that time. The keel[4] was laid on 7th September, 1957.

On 11th May, 1960, nearly three years later, I was first blessed by the Bishop of Nantes upon completion. I was launched by Madame Yvonne de Gaulle, wife of Charles de Gaulle – President of France – at 4.15 pm and given the name "*SS France*". Around 4.22 pm, I was afloat in the sea on my tugs. De Gaulle, who was present at the inauguration, made an emotional patriotic speech. He recalled the *SS Normandie* and said he saw a new *Normandie* in me, bringing pride to France. This is the first time that I heard the name *Normandie*. More than a year later, on 19th November, 1961, I undertook my trial voyage.

Trial voyage

The voyage was scheduled to depart from Le Havre,[5] destined for the Canary Islands.[6] It took me nine days: from 19th to 27th January, 1962. I had 1700 passengers aboard, including dignitaries like Mrs and Mr De Gaulle. Everybody was exceedingly cheerful. They all felt privileged to be the first passengers to step onto a passenger liner destined to make France proud. Though few shortcomings were noticed during the trial voyage, overall, there was satisfaction. I was declared fit for my maiden voyage across the seas.

Incidentally, it was during this short trial voyage that I had a glimpse of the *SS Liberte'*–another ocean liner–gracefully sailing on her way to a shipbreaking yard. This had been one name that had kept me in awe. I was curious to know more about her and why she was going forward to embrace her death. During my voyages, I kept my ears open and mind alert so that I didn't miss any conversation relating to the *Normandie* and the *Liberte'*. I also learnt that two earlier French ships had also been named *France*. Even during the trial voyage, there was a lot of discussion about these historic ships, enough to make my maiden voyage significant.

SS France (1896) and *SS France* (1912)

I trust you will not mind if I take a short break from my story at this juncture and tell you some stories of who my great predecessors were. It would make the narration of my first maiden voyage more meaningful and you would also be able to place me correctly in the historical context. Let me start with my namesake, the *France* ocean liners. I will be brief, be assured.

The first *SS France* was constructed in 1896 at the Forges & Chantiers shipyard in La Seyne, France. On 7th November, 1915, during World War I, while she was on a voyage from Mudros, Greece, to Marseille, France, she was shelled by the German submarine SM *U-38* in the Mediterranean Sea near the coast of Sardinia. The ocean liner suffered several explosions and fires. Fortunately, the crew and passengers were able to abandon the ship and there were no casualties. She sank a few hours later.

The second *SS France* was built at Chantiers de l'Atlantique St. Nazaire in 1912. She was launched into the river Loire in September 1910 with great joy and applause. After work on her beautiful interiors had been completed, she commenced her maiden voyage from Le Havre to New York on 20th April, 1912. If you remember something about that date, please note that it was just five days after the *Titanic*[7] sank. The *Titanic* tragedy made an initial dent in the popularity of the second *SS France,* to begin with, but quite soon she became very popular in the Atlantic. Her lavish interiors earned her the nickname "Versailles of the Atlantic"—a reference to the Palace of Versailles - a former royal residence built by King Louis XIV at Versailles, a town about 19 kilometres west of Paris. During World War I, *France* served as a hospital ship and also ferried troops. She returned to Le Havre in 1919. Except for a brief period, she served till September 1932, carrying out her final voyage on 9th September, 1932. Her retirement was announced during the voyage itself. She was scrapped at Dunkirk, a coastal city in northern France, in 1935. Her place was taken by the *SS Normandie*.

When passengers aboard discussed the tragedy of the *Titanic*, they did not fail to refer to the misfortunes of one Laroche family. Their travel was originally booked on the *SS France.* As the ship management conveyed to them that their children would not be allowed to eat in the dining room with the adults, the family rebooked its passage on the *Titanic*, set to sail a week earlier. Sadly, Mr Laroche lost his life in the *Titanic* tragedy.

SS Normandie–the Ship of Lights

There were many ocean liners in existence much before my birth, as I told you, but if I have to name one of whom I am truly proud of, it would be the *SS Normandie*. The praise lavished on the *Normandie* by a person none less than Charles De Gaulle made me think with pride and adoration about my predecessors. It is always good to remember one's lineage as it humbles you with gratitude and encourages you to come up in life.

The *SS Normandie* was named after the French Province of Normandie in the north of France, known for its beautiful landscapes. The *Normandie* earned

SS Normandie, the ship of lights

the reputation of being the greatest ocean liner ever built and it was a legend in its class. She was indeed the ultimate ocean liner.

The circumstances in which *SS Normandie* took birth were extremely disturbing. The First World War (1914-1918) was just over, and people were trying hard to recover from the devastation it had caused. The onset of the Great Depression[8] made conditions worse. Despite the stock market crash of 1929, a Frenchman decided to build an ocean liner that would compete with all the others and bring a name to France. The Government of France even agreed to provide a subsidy when requested by the French builder. As such, the endeavour was considered important in the national interest.

Interestingly, this great ocean liner did not have a name when its construction began on 26th January, 1931 at Saint Nazaire, France. The French could not decide whether the name should have a masculine prefix '*le*'–like all their other French ships–or '*la*', the feminine prefix, just to please prospective wealthy American clients. To avoid any controversy, the *SS Normandie* was left without any prefix. It was like the Greek God Hermaphroditus,[9] who is depicted as being both male and female. Nonetheless, the owners did install an eight-foot-high bronze sculpture of a woman named '*La Normandie*', at the top of its grand stairway. With all the beauty and charm that *Normandie* possessed and its sleek feminine look, it seems unfair not to have given her the honour of the prefix '*La*'. Not a gender bias, but I seek liberty to say what my view is. Pardon me for taking this poetic liberty!

The *SS Normandie* was launched on 29th October, 1932 in the presence of a huge audience. Albert Lebrun,[10] the President of France, Madam Lebrun and other dignitaries graced the occasion. The Loire River must have felt the enormous presence and weight of the magnificent ship. Though weighing over 80,000 tons and measuring around 1000 feet, she was still the fastest and smoothest ocean liner ever built. The day of her first maiden voyage soon arrived. She left Le Havre for New York on 29th May, 1935 and completed the journey in a record time of 4 days, 3 hours and 14 minutes. The *Normandie* broke all earlier records and won the prestigious Blue Riband.[11] It was a great honour for France as this was the first time that one of its ocean liners had received this distinction. The *Normandie* travelled the world for over five years (from 1935 to 1940). She made 139 crossings between Europe and the United States, and two trips to Rio de Janeiro.

The ship's fame and finery attracted the elites of all societies. The list of celebrities who travelled on the *Normandie* included, among others, famous authors and personalities including, Ernest Hemingway, P.G. Wodehouse, Marlene Dietrich, Walt Disney, Douglas Fairbanks, Jr. James Stewart, Bing Crosby and the Von Trapp Family Singers (of *Sound of Music* fame). In the list of celebrities, I also noticed the name of Salvador Dali–a well-known Spanish artist. I have many interesting stories of my own to relate about him when he travelled with me.

One of the reasons why celebrities were attracted to *Normandie* was her sheer luxurious look and exotic interiors, beautifully adorned with paintings and sculptures. There were chandeliers in every room, Lalique pillars for illumination and a magnificent dining hall that could accommodate 157 tables with 700 seats. Obviously, the builders of the *Normandie* had focussed almost exclusively on the comfort and luxuries of its first-class passengers by sequestering the maximum space for them. No wonder she was called the 'Ship of Lights'–just as Paris, in those days, was called the 'City of Lights'!

I must share with you a few special features about the *Normandie*. Its hydrodynamic hull–designed by Vladimir Yourkevitch, a famous ship architect, who was earlier in the Russian Navy but later emigrated to France – was unique. Another important feature was its radar – a piece of equipment missing on the *Titanic* and which contributed to its doom.

The grand dining hall of *SS Normandie*

Not everything about the *Normandie*, however, evoked praise. Too much attention had been paid by its designers to the needs of its wealthy clients; consequently, the second and tourist classes suffered. The *Normandie,* in fact, was branded as a ship only for 'the rich and the famous' and eventually became unpopular with its Atlantic passengers. Its contemporaries, such as the *RMS Queen Mary*[12], did not face this problem, as they had allotted proper space to all the passengers, including those travelling by second and tourist class. But it was neither possible nor did the reputation gained by the *Normandie* permit it to compromise with its standards. The result was that it had to travel half-empty many times and its earnings could barely cover the running costs. In fact, for this very reason, its owners were never able to repay the loan from the French Government that had made her construction possible. Apart from this criticism–which emerged from a different point of view–nobody who travelled with me ever uttered a word against her grandeur and glory or questioned her position as one of the greatest ocean liners of all time. The *Normandie* went on to win the Blue Riband five times: twice westbound, thrice eastbound.

Now we come to the sad part.

The outbreak of the Second World War (1939-1945) brought an interruption to Atlantic travel in 1940. As a consequence, and as the Germans invaded France and seized Paris, the *Normandie*, which had arrived in New York on 28th August 1939 never sailed again. Along with her competitor, the *Queen Mary*, she was interned by the Americans in New York Port. The war took over the entire world. The *Normandie* had no option but to sit idle at Pier 88 on the West Side of Manhattan at 48th Street, waiting for the day that she could go back to her homeland. Alas! this was never to be. In 1941, as Japan dropped bombs on the ships docked at Pearl Harbour[13] and America officially joined World War II, *Normandie* lost her citizenship, her identity and all her

The U.S.S. "Lafayette," formerly the S.S. "Normandie," catching fire in New York Harbor, February 9, 1942. National Archives.

finery. The liner was claimed by the American Navy on 7th December, 1941. It ceased to be the proud French liner it once was but would be converted into an American troop ship called the *USS Lafayette*. The Americans must be given credit, however, for acknowledging the *Normandie's* French roots by renaming it after the Marquis de La Fayette[14]–the French general who had fought in the American Revolutionary War.

Then arrived a fate worse than death.

On 9th February, 1942, as the people of New York watched helplessly in the cold winter afternoon, the *Normandie* went up in flames. It was reported that the fire started from a careless welder's torch while *Normandie* was being hastily stripped of her worthless finery in order to convert it into a troop transporter. Some even proposed sabotage by German foes. One section of mobsters claimed the responsibility of sabotage but no sabotage was ever proved. Later, after a government investigation, it was found that the fire was purely accidental.

The ship blazed for twelve hours: thick plumes of black smoke covered the sun and spread across the city's skyline. Though all possible efforts were made to douse the flames, none were successful. Vladimir Yourkevitch – the ship's designer – came up with a plan to prevent the vessel from capsizing. Rear Admiral Adolphus Andrews – the naval commander in charge–rejected the plan. Injured workers were rushed to the hospital.

Finally, after twelve hours of fire-fighting and crowds watching the spectacle in mute horror, the fire died out. By then, the ship had rolled over to the bottom of the river Hudson. She remained at the bottom of the Hudson for a year and a half. Thereafter, with some basic repairs, she was refloated in 1943 but declared unsalvageable and towed to Brooklyn Naval Yard. She died a cruel death when she was broken up for scrap in October 1946 at Port Newark, New Jersey.

It is said that the *SS Normandie* was constructed at a cost of $60 million but after it was dismantled, it was sold as scrap at $3.80 a ton! The ship that had charmed everyone for years was gone. Nobody could have imagined that a ship once known as the Pride of France would suffer this inglorious end at some other country's port!

It saddens me, but no one has control over destiny. In that sense, we are all bound, not free to choose. In France, lovers of the *Normandie* still go to any extent to acquire even a tiny scrap of her. They still talk about her–stories and gossip–but, at times, tinged with nostalgia. A hotel in Florida still proudly displays, as I am told, the eight-foot-high bronze sculpture of the woman named '*La Normandie*' from the ship, reminding everyone of the great legacy she has left behind.

SS Europa to *SS Liberte'*

I had only heard about the SS *Normandie* but never met her. But I did meet another grand ship—the *SS Liberte',* initially known as the *SS Europa,* which served as a passenger liner in France from 1950 for at least a decade. My meeting with her on the trans-Atlantic route was by sheer chance. As I have related earlier, I was on my trial voyage to the Canary Islands, whereas she was slowly but gracefully sailing to embrace her end at Le Spezia – an Italian ship breaking yard. I gazed at her and imagined how grand and beautiful she must have been in her youth. Passengers gathered at my deck looked at the *SS Liberte'* with awe and surprise. Some (perhaps they knew) were quite sad. For days they kept talking about her. I listened attentively to them and am merely narrating here whatever little facts I could glean from their conversations.

There is another important connection between the *Liberte'* and the *Normandie*: After the Second World War ended, the *Liberte'* was handed over by the Reparation Commission[15] to France as war compensation for the loss of the *SS Normandie* at New York.

The first thing which immediately springs to everyone's mind when hearing about the *SS Liberte'* was her prominent role in the Jane Russel musical film–*The French Line* (1954). She became world-famous, however, in *Sabrina* starring Humphrey Bogart and Audrey Hepburn. The passengers I listened to also talked about her being a favourite of the celebrities of those days travelling between the United States and Europe, and mentioned the names of William Randolph Hearst–the newspaper magnate, Parisian fashion designer Elsa Schiaparelli, opera star Madame Elizabeth Rethberg and industrialists like the steel giant Charles M. Schwab, among others. But at the same time, I was sad to hear about her life's journey which appeared to be full of trials and tribulations. It happens with some for reasons unknown. Destiny plays different roles with different people, irrespective of the best efforts made by each one of them.

The journey of *Europa*, as she was then known, began in Germany, which had a long history of keeping luxury liners. These liners were lost in the First

World War. Soon, however, the passion for building liners returned, resulting in the birth of the *SS Europa* and her sister, the *SS Bremen*. The *Europa* was supposed to be launched before the *Bremen.* Her construction ought to have been over by the spring of 1929. But the first tragedy struck on the morning of 26th March, 1929: the vessel caught fire for reasons which could not be ascertained. The fire raged throughout the day. It was only by the evening that it was brought under control. By then, her turbines had suffered serious damage. Repairs were carried out, no doubt at considerable cost. Her damaged hull was fixed and she was ready for voyage by February 1930. By this time, however, the *SS Bremen* had already been launched (August 1928). Finally, on 19th March, 1930, the *Europa* commenced her maiden voyage from Hamburg to New York. She crossed the Atlantic in a record time of 4 days, 17 hours and 6 minutes at an unprecedented average cruising speed of 27.91 knots. This feat earned her the Blue Riband, which she held for three years before it was reclaimed by the *Bremen* in June 1933.

The *Europa's* funnels were designed to be of low height in order to enhance her overall profile and to complement her sleek contours. But they were not appreciated by her passengers who found themselves too close to her sooty smoke. This problem was soon resolved by raising the funnels by another 15 feet. A unique feature was shared both by the *Europa* and the *Bremen*: each had a small catapult[16] on its upper deck. Using the catapult, the Germans launched the aircraft 'Heinkel He 58 D-1919 Bremen Atlantic' from the Europa's upper deck. The aircraft flew from the ship to a port in Blixen. Although the catapult was later abandoned for being too costly and cumbersome, it became a stepping stone towards what would become formidable German military capabilities in the imminent Second World War. Adolf Hitler wanted Germany to regain the pride it had lost in the First World War. He, therefore, wanted to use the *Europa* as a naval accommodation ship. The *Europa's* last journey as a passenger ship was on 10th August, 1939 before she was painted grey and moored at Bremerhaven to serve as a command post for the German Navy. Hitler chose her for the planned invasion of Great Britain which was dubbed 'Operation Sea Lion'[17]. The operation was, however, abandoned in October 1940 and the *Europa* was back at Bremerhaven. History records this as a major blunder committed by Hitler. Instead of attacking an unprepared England, he chose to attack powerful Russia. The US Army–which was advancing towards Germany–reached Bremerhaven in 1945 and captured the *Europa*. The war

SS Europa

ended a few weeks later. On 8th May, 1945 the United States claimed the ship as a war prize and handed it over to its Navy.

The US Navy commissioned her on 25th August, 1945, giving her a new name–the *USS Europa* and a new identity–that of a troopship used for repatriation. She travelled between the UK and the US ferrying many American soldiers back home. The war had left only poverty and destruction behind. The *USS Europa* with her cheap replacement fittings, soon began to suffer and show signs of distress. Minor fires besieged her journeys. Cracks were also discovered in her hull. The ship sailed on its last voyage on 15th March, 1946 from New York for Kirkwall in the Orkney Islands,[18] Scotland – a journey she could not, in fact, complete. She was decommissioned on 2nd May 1946 and anchored at Bremerhaven. The Reparation Commission had given the *Europa* to France as war compensation for the loss of *Normandie* at New York. The French Line *Compaigne Générale Transatlantique* took over the ownership of the vessel and brought it to Le Havre to be used in place of the *Normandie*. She was repainted with her funnel red and her tops black. As luck would have it, on December 8, 1946, due to bad weather, she broke from her anchorage and collided head-on with the wreckage of another ship –

the *Paris*[19]– which had capsized beside her at Le Havre. Her fractured hull now had a gaping hole and she was trapped in a mudbank. However, in the absence of any replacement yet for the *Normandie* and because of the lasting French love for liners, she was shipped off to the famous Chantiers de l'Atlantique shipyard in Saint-Nazaire for repairs.

But the bad days were hardly over.

Once again fire broke out on the ship in October 1949. This time, her passenger space was damaged. Optimistic as the French are – and a little crazy about ships–the *Europa* was rebuilt after spending another 19 million dollars and five years of labour. With new vigour and vitality, she made her maiden voyage to New York on 2nd August, 1950 under the new name, the *SS Liberte'*. She spent eleven years as the star of the French fleet, carrying passengers between Le Havre and New York.

But soon the *Liberte'* started losing her charm. She looked old and was no longer attractive to the rich and the famous. I got this impression from the conversations of passengers who ventured the opinion that my advent as a passenger liner was one of the reasons for her abandonment. Sad, I thought. How could human beings be so selfish? How can one abandon those who served for years so easily?

SS Liberte'

The *SS Liberte'* made her final voyage in 1962 and finally bowed out in 1963 at La Spezia, the Italian ship breaking yard. It was while on this final journey, as I said earlier, that I saw her for the first and the last time. After hearing her story from the passengers, I was tense for a moment. Was this going to be my fate as well? But soon, I reminded myself that I have no control over the future – none whatsoever – when I am chosen for a voyage on the vast and limitless sea. I must learn to live in the present. We all have to learn this, willingly or unwillingly.

PART-II
Meeting Mona Lisa

Back to my story: My maiden voyage

You must be eager to have me resume the telling of my story. I will commence from the point I had left off. So, after the trial voyage, I was to take the maiden crossing from *Le Havre* to the Port of New York, covering a distance of 3,662 nautical miles and passing through the English Channel, the Bay of Biscay and the North Atlantic Ocean. The dates were already fixed: 3rd - 8th February, 1962.

The journey commenced on the afternoon of 3rd February with Commandant Georges Croisile in charge. Among others, Ms Yvonne de Gaulle, wife of the French President, was also on board in her official capacity as godmother of the ship. Juliette Greco, a young actress, was also a passenger. The Atlantic is quite harsh in February. Its waves surged 45 feet and one broke a glass window and eight bottles of scotch. That was not a good sign. The vessel's speed immediately slowed. But I reached New York Port safely, as scheduled, on 8th February. It was bitterly cold outside, but the welcome was extremely warm, with cheers all around. As fate would have it, I was anchored at Pier 88, where the *SS Normandie* had been chained twenty years ago (minus a day). It was the place where the *SS Normandie* had also caught fire and sank – the place of her doom. And here I was, anchored at the exact same spot, at the very beginning of my career! What an irony! A shadow of gloom descended but soon disappeared in the loud cheers of the gathering that had assembled to greet me. A blast of fresh air touched me and I felt refreshed.

One interesting anecdote is worth recounting. Someone who was habituated to finding faults with everything, hazarded the opinion that the ship was too large to transit through the Panama canal. When he heard it, de Gaulle–

in his inimitable manner–retorted: 'The ship is not too big; the problem is that the canal is too small!'

Mona Lisa–The enigma

As I said at the beginning of this tale, I don't wish to go chronologically with my voyages as I am eager to recount for you the most exciting moments of my life on the seas. Not that the other events are less important, but if I am asked to rank them all, I would place at the top of the list, without a second thought, my travel with da Vinci's *Mona Lisa*.

You may be wondering why the famous *Mona Lisa*[20] (*La Gioconda,* if we use her popular Italian name) was brought to *Le Havre*, where I was anchored, waiting for my next voyage. What happened was quite dramatic. On 14th December, 1962, I noticed unusual activity at the berth: a convoy safeguarding a truck with a squadron of six police motorcycles suddenly arrived alongside. It appeared to be a secret mission. I could see a wooden crate–covering a metal box–being offloaded very carefully from the truck. I was nervous: was this a nuclear weapon? And why was a passenger ship chosen for this purpose?

Slowly and carefully, the box was brought on board and taken to Cabin M-79. It was draped in a thick dark-grey wool blanket. Nobody was allowed to step near the cabin. There were nine French guards and two officials from the Louvre watching Cabin-79 all the time. All the passengers were intrigued and excited. An air of suspicion hung over the ship and various kinds of rumours were floated. Curious, I was also keeping my eyes and ears open to the conversations.

The captain of the ship, however, could not hold on to the secret for too long.

He soon announced with great fanfare that the great *Mona Lisa* was travelling with them on the journey up to New York. There was loud cheering. Suddenly, the silent and suspicious atmosphere turned into festivity. People started celebrating the news – they danced, burst into songs and champagne bottles opened. The chefs prepared special dishes: "Mona Lisa pastry", "Mona Lisa salad".

And then the guess work with individual imaginations started to run riot. Different theories floated around as to how all this happened. It was a proud and special moment for me. I could not imagine in my wildest dreams that one day, the *Mona Lisa* – the lady with the enigmatic smile – would travel with me.

Heavily guarded *Mona Lisa* arrived in New York on December 19, 1962

My eyes remained fixed on Cabin M-79, which was under strict surveillance. People kept on trying to peep or gawk as if they would somehow be fortunate to get a glimpse of the *Mona Lisa.* Inside, the almost 500-year-old charming lady—wholly unaware of the outside world—slept comfortably in her cabin, with the temperature ideally maintained. A well-intentioned passenger, thinking that the *Mona Lisa* might step out barefoot and hurt herself, even risked the tight security to place a pair of sandals outside the cabin!

I listened attentively to the conversations and also gathered numerous other pieces of information in all these years about this magnificent piece of art. I can now tell you the story in great detail. Briefly, Jacqueline Kennedy[21] – 'Jackie' as she was popularly called – was extremely fond of French art and literature. She also had a degree in French literature. On 31st May, 1961, when John F. Kennedy was on a presidential visit to Paris, less than six months after taking office, Jacqueline, his wife, accompanied him. The author of *La Condition Humaine,* Andre Malraux,[22] was then France's Cultural Minister. Malraux was a charismatic personality. Jackie had read his book and was keen to meet him. They met and Malraux personally took Jackie on a tour of the famous art places of Paris.

Deeply impressed by his sophistication and knowledge, and soon after her return, Jackie saw to it that Malraux received an official invitation to visit Washington. After an initial hesitation, Malraux finally agreed to come to the USA in May 1962. Jackie greeted him warmly at the National Gallery. At some stage during their conversation, it appears, Jackie proposed that Malraux consider loaning the *Mona Lisa* to America for a short while so that Americans too could get to view this great piece of art. Malraux did not commit but apparently said, 'I will see what I can do.'

That day itself, in the afternoon, Edward Folliard, a reporter with the *Washington Post*, wrote: 'Wouldn't it be wonderful if the *Mona Lisa* could be shown at the National Gallery?' The news quoted Malraux to the effect that France felt that these masterpieces belonged to mankind. That day, in honour of Malraux, Jackie arranged for a dinner, where she invited several celebrities, including painter Mark Rothko and writers Thornton Wilder, Tennessee Williams and Saul Bellow, among others. After dinner, she got a commitment from Malraux that the *Mona Lisa* would be sent as a loan to Mrs and Mr Kennedy. Undoubtedly, it was the charm and persuasive abilities of Jackie that succeeded in making the visit of the *Mona Lisa* to the US possible.

This is just a brief historical background to the arrival of the great masterpiece to the US. I don't want to enter into the gossip which also floated in the press, that Jackie had an "intellectual crush" on Malraux and that, at some point after dinner, she was seen sitting so close to him that her right shoulder nearly touched his arm. These pieces of gossip are very often introduced to trigger the immense capacity of mankind to imagine even the unimaginable!

But execution of this idea was not going to be easy. The world was on the cusp of a nuclear war. Russia had installed its missiles in Cuba to attack America. Kennedy had warned Nikita Khrushchev of a total naval blockade. US missiles had already been moved to Turkey. On 28th October, 1962, Khrushchev could be persuaded to dismantle Russia's installations in Cuba to launch missiles. In reciprocation, Kennedy also agreed to move the US missiles out of Turkey. These historic decisions eased the tension a bit.

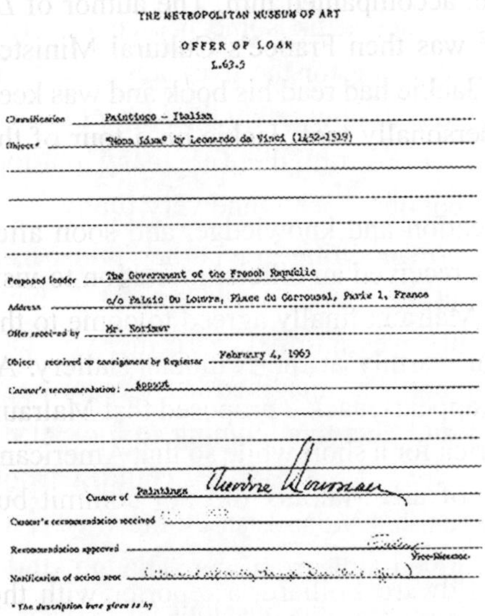

THE METROPOLITAN MUSEUM OF ART

OFFER OF LOAN

L.63.5

Classification: Paintings – Italian

Object*: "Mona Lisa" by Leonardo da Vinci (1452–1519)

Proposed lender: The Government of the French Republic

Address: c/o Palais Du Louvre, Place du Carrousel, Paris 1, France

Offer received by: Mr. Rorimer

Object received on consignment by Registrar: February 4, 1963

Curator's recommendation: Accept

Curator of: Paintings

Curator's recommendation received

Recommendation approved

Vice-Director.

Notification of action sent

* The description here given is by

Offer of loan by the Metropolitan Museum of Art

Notwithstanding the tense situation, however, preparations were going ahead to move the masterpiece from the Louvre[23] in Paris. Once the proposal made it to the French media, people in Paris became agitated and angry. There were angry demonstrations in the streets. Editorials were written denouncing the lending. Some art lovers called the proposal to take the *Mona Lisa* in a wooden frame across the Atlantic Ocean, insane. Headlines shouted: "*La Jaconde must not leave the Louvre.*"

The attachment of the French people to this precious painting must be understood. It is one of the greatest artworks of all time. It is easily the greatest attraction of the Louvre, France's most well-known museum. But the *Mona Lisa* became an obsession after the notorious incident of its theft that took place, which is marked as the greatest art theft of the twentieth century. An employee of the Louvre had stolen the masterpiece in August 1911. After a world-wide search, it was recovered in Italy, where the said employee–Vincenzo Peruggia[24]–was caught trying to sell it to an art dealer. Being aware of these protests and the sentiments of the French people, Madam Jackie in Washington was frantically preparing for the absolute care and security of this great treasure. It was decided to put it in a vault with independent air-conditioning and to take all steps to protect it from any kind of tremors or jerks.

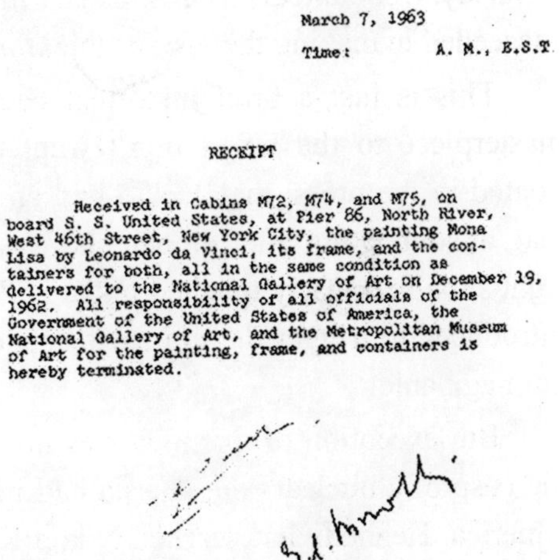

March 7, 1963

Time: A. M., E.S.T.

RECEIPT

Received in Cabins M72, M74, and M75, on board S. S. United States, at Pier 86, North River, West 46th Street, New York City, the painting Mona Lisa by Leonardo da Vinci, its frame, and the containers for both, all in the same condition as delivered to the National Gallery of Art on December 19, 1962. All responsibility of all officials of the Government of the United States of America, the National Gallery of Art, and the Metropolitan Museum of Art for the painting, frame, and containers is hereby terminated.

Return receipt for the Mona Lisa. Office of the Secretary Records, The Metropolitan Museum of Art

Finally, on 14th December, 1962, this historic journey began. I started sailing around 3.15 pm from Le Havre, picked up some passengers from Southampton and then plunged into the Atlantic for the five-days journey to America. I have already given you some idea of how safely the *Mona Lisa* was being transported. But besides the above serious stuff, there are many hilarious stories. I don't wish to recount them except one that I found very funny.

Amidst all this merriment, I heard a man sitting in a corner, whispering to a lady nearby: 'What is so great about the *Mona Lisa*? To me, she looks so ordinary!' and then added, pouring his eyes into hers: 'To me, you look no less!' Her face brimmed. For a moment, she imagined her picture being tucked on a wall above the *Mona Lisa* and everyone coming to look at her instead, ignoring the *Mona Lisa*! Poor *Mona Lisa*!! But if I could, I would have asked Leonardo da Vinci – who was this Mona Lisa by the way? I am not sure whether da Vinci would have given a clear answer. Though stories float around who she was. I think in creation, the subconscious takes over the creative urge without the artist's knowledge and at the end he himself marvels at his own creation. That is how sometimes a masterpiece is created–whether it is painting, music or poetry. Oh! I am not learned. Surely not. I have picked all this up from the company of learned people and their conversations. I was, of course, a little jealous during those days because all talk afloat was about the

People waiting in front of the Museum to see the *Mona Lisa*

Elevated view facing west with people waiting in line to see the *Mona Lisa*

Mona Lisa and no one was admiring me! A little ego, or jealousy, I suppose, is not bad! I agree that one should be careful so that it does not become an obsession.

I am told that the lending of the *Mona Lisa* to America served France politically and brought national pride to it. Though not recognized as such politically, the event certainly conveyed a message of goodwill at the international level.

I entered New York harbour in the morning of 19th December, 1962 and docked at Pier 88. As I was carrying the *Mona Lisa* on board, it was my time to display attitude. I had a sleek body and a grand look. It was flattering to see the huge warm welcome by hundreds of people and passengers standing at the decks waving scarves and flags. It was nearly an hour's celebration. I saw Jean Chatelain, the French Director General of Museums, handing over the

JFK, André Malraux, Jackie and others unveiling *Mona Lisa* at National Gallery of Art

responsibility for safe keeping of the *Mona Lisa* to John Walker, Director of the Washington-based National Gallery of Art, on behalf of President Kennedy. I came to know later that the *Mona Lisa* was escorted under huge security arrangements to the National Gallery. All traffic along the route was halted. The *Mona Lisa*, in fact, received the level of secret service protection that is normally reserved for the President of the United States! On 8th January, 1963, every member of Kennedy's Cabinet, all sitting U.S. Senators and Congressmen, as well as all the nine justices of the US Supreme Court, were present at the ceremony held at the National Gallery where the painting was to be put on public display. What a great honour and respect paid to the *Mona Lisa*!

The *Mona Lisa* stayed on display at the National Gallery of Art for some time. Thereafter, she was sent to the Metropolitan Museum of Art in New York, where she went on display on 6th February, 1963. A long line of eager Americans was already waiting since early morning to have a glimpse of her. A taxi driver from Brooklyn said he had been waiting since 4.30 am to have a view of this mysterious woman. No admission fee was charged. The weekday hours for viewing the painting were extended up to 9 pm. Over a million visitors saw the *Mona Lisa*. The one-millionth visitor was one Arthur Pomerantz of New Rochelle who was given a reproduction of the painting and gifts for his children. It is recorded that on one of the days, 63,675 people were received by the Museum.

One scary event occurred at the Museum which could have led to the destruction of the painting. The incident was connected with the activation of the fire sprinklers one night. The tragedy was averted because the thick glass covering the painting acted like a protective shield. Nothing happened to the *Mona Lisa*. It was safe. After all, she had the mysterious aura to absorb many such incidents, accidents and conspiracies! The incident was hushed up by the museum authorities.

People still remember the passionate speech given by Kennedy at the National Museum on the occasion: "*Politics and art, the life of action and the life of thought, the world of events and the world of imagination, are one.*" The French Ambassador to the United States, Harve Alphand, also had something interesting to say during the unveiling ceremony on 6th February at the Metropolitan Museum. He described the *Mona Lisa* as an extraordinary painting depicting the 'mystery of human creativity'. While many admirers sent her love letters, those who questioned her charm and beauty pasted a moustache on her face!

The grand welcome accorded to the *Mona Lisa* in the United States silenced Malraux's critics. I came to know that the exhibition of the painting was finally closed on 4th March, 1963. On 7th March, it boarded the *SS United States* for its journey back to France. The *Mona Lisa* reached the Louvre after an uneventful voyage on 12th March. I was not fortunate enough to ferry her back to France; it would have been a great privilege, of course. But after she left me for the museum on 19th December, 1962, I also left New York, this time with a heavy heart, but preserving all her memories and the honour she had brought to me. Just eight months thereafter, on 22nd November, 1963, I heard passengers talking about the assassination of Kennedy at Dallas, Texas. The news was quite disturbing and made me feel sad for many days.

If you don't mind, may I continue with the recounting of another wonderful experience? Does it not happen that once you are involved with a particular subject of your liking, you want to remain in that mood for some more time? I have already told you the story of the young man who would play the violin at night on the deck. I admired him hugely. I saw another man, not so young, who loved singing. He was not a great singer but he had a melodious voice. He would sit somewhere in a corner of the ship and sing for several hours, not caring whether anybody was listening to him or not. I like such

Mona Lisa by Leonardo da Vinci

people. They give society a lot but remain blissfully ignorant about their contribution. There is no desire in them to earn praise. No ego. But I am not like that. I want you to listen to me and to pay attention to my narrative. I am, as I told you, reaching my end and have yet to tell you of many things. I am, of course, not like one of those who are constantly seeking some company. If you are quietly sitting by their side, they will not hesitate a bit to ask you: Who are you? What do you do? etc., and thus obstruct you from enjoying your own company. Oh, one's life's span is long and, therefore, people have to find ways to while away their time, either by talking or by listening–but rarely by being alone with themselves. Another interesting thing that I heard was a man on the ship telling someone, "See, I talk a lot because I know so much. Others are jealous because they don't know much and therefore, don't speak!" Wonderful world! Wonderful people!

Salvadore Dali–the master of surrealism

I had a gala time for thirteen years; lots of people, festivities, marriages, love affairs, music and dance. I had virtually forgotten every other thing. Day and night, unending activities continued. I was very happy. It was a matter of pride for anyone to travel with me. I was in the prime of my youth and I wished that this beautiful dream would never end. From 1962 to 1974, I did 377 trans-Atlantic crossings, 91 cruises, and two world tours and carried 1,13,862 passengers.

It was on one of these journeys in the 1970s that the master of surrealism[25], Salvador Dali[26], came on board and travelled with me. He must have been a frequent traveller as he had also been on the *Normandie*. What news he made there, I am not aware, but he must have been attracted by my fame. He, therefore, came with Gala, his wife, Captain Moore and Babou, his pet–an ocelot[27] or dwarf leopard! Dali would move around with ocelot on the ship, creating panic among the passengers. The captain of the ship, somehow, kept on assuring the passengers that the ocelot would not harm anybody. From the conversations, I came to know that Dali had acquired this pet in the year 1960 from a Colombian chief. For the children on board, all this of course was great fun. I heard (please don't mind my continuous eavesdropping) what passengers said about surrealism. Many searched dictionaries for its meaning. One man said that it was something like 'quarrying the unconscious'–digging out material and presenting it before the people in a certain disorder! Dali had pointed moustaches, which people said acted like antennas to receive signals from aliens! It seems that the source of his creative (wild) dreams was '*Camembert*'–a kind of cheese–which he was accustomed to consume in huge quantities before going to bed. Over and above all this, he created his individual perfume, wearing cow dung and fish glue! I conjectured (my own weird guess) that he must be applying fish glue to his moustache and spraying the cow dung perfume on himself! I think all this was done to maintain his aura of individuality. I really pitied his wife. Of course, the pet must have enjoyed his company! I came to know later that for his wife, he had created a "surrealist scent", a concoction of jasmine and rose. It was contained in a bottle which Dali had himself designed. The bottle had a nose and lips. After all, for Dali, the sense of smell "best gives the idea of immortality." It appears that in his youth, sometime in 1938, he met Sigmund Freud, who at that time was nearly 82. When Dali was drawing his sketch, it is said that Freud remarked: "This boy looks like a lunatic." I heard many passengers whispering his famous statement: "Every morning upon awakening, I experience a supreme pleasure, that of being Salvador Dali!" To me, his very personality was very mysterious–beyond my imagination. Whenever I looked at him, I found his entire persona exhibiting surrealism, as if continuous massive digging of the unconscious was going on! In any case, it was difficult for me to understand these subtle concepts. The entire story surrounding Dali was so amusing to me that it made me laugh and laugh. Never thereafter have

Salvadore Dali and Ocelot

I laughed so much! Good that Dali did not see me; otherwise, he would have felt offended.

I must tell you another interesting incident. There was a fan of Dali who came to know about the so-called secret of his creativity. So before going to bed, he ate lots of Camembert. The next day, he was seen in the doctor's chamber complaining of loose motions! Lesson to be learnt: It is not wise to imitate others! If body and mind are not ready, creativity can be the most dangerous purgative, taking one from doctors to even an asylum! Dali was happy with the ocelot, but who knew about the happiness of the ocelot itself, which had been taken away from its natural habitat? Ocelots became an endangered species and, therefore, had to be released. Carlos Lozano, an actor and Dali's friend, mentions in his memoirs that "I saw the ocelot smile only once, the day it was released."

With this, I end the story of Salvador Dali's journey with me. If my narration has evoked some interest, you may read his books–from cooking to nuclear mysticism, see his paintings and enjoy the controversies and interesting stories surrounding his life. As far as I remember, during the entire journey, Dali did not paint a single picture. I was told that a famous painting, '*Lady Blue–The High Priestess*' was done by him in 1979. But that must have been something different because I was given the name *Blue Lady* much later.

Many other celebrities also travelled with me. David Bowie, a famous English singer and actor, boarded me for a voyage in 1974. Cary Grant, a famous film actor, also embarked with me on a trip. Coincidentally, he had also travelled on the *SS Normandie* and the *SS Europa*. Michel Sardou,[28] a well-known French singer and songwriter who had also travelled with me, wrote a song '*Le France*' in 1975, criticising Valery Giscard d'Estaing, the then President of France for withdrawing me from service. The song was: "Don't call me France again!" Let me also mention the names of other well-known personalities whose company I was privileged to enjoy: Johnny Halliday (French rock & roll singer and actor), Audrey Hepburn (British actress), the Beatles (rock band), Andy Warhol (American artist, film director and producer), Paul Morrissey (American film director) and Tennessee Williams (American playwright).

You can imagine the abundant joy of floating around all the time, piercing the cold silence of the dark sea and listening to praise after praise. It gave a feeling that nothing would change and that the songs, dances and merriment would continue forever!

PART-III

Turn of events

The Descent of Dark Shadows

Events first commenced casting their dark shadows around 1973. These events may have actually started taking place at the beginning of 1970 itself. But when everything is going right, you tend to ignore negative signs. It is natural. Around 1970, jet travel became more popular than travel by ship. But things did not appear too bad for me. Even in 1972, I did two world travels and was very happy. In fact, in1973, I became the largest passenger ship in the world by default, because my competitor, the *RMS Queen Elizabeth*[29], was destroyed that year in a fire in Hong Kong.

The year 1973 also produced the oil crisis. The price of oil and fuel skyrocketed. It shot up from \$3 to \$12 per barrel. The French government calculated that to run a passenger ship like mine, it would have to shell out an additional \$10 million a year. Therefore, without a subsidy, it would not be possible to continue with my service. Accordingly, the government issued a press release in which it declared that it was withdrawing me from service effective from 25th October, 1974.

I could not believe the news when I first heard it. I was in good condition, healthy and could have served the French nation for many more years. But the times were changing. People who had seen me as the pride of France were either no longer alive or had started taking interest in air travel. If many like-minded people had come together, they could have found out ways and means to make my travels sustainable. But no one came to my rescue. Unlike the events surrounding my birth, this time there were no parliamentary debates, no discussions, no planning! There were only a handful of people who appeared unhappy. I felt deeply hurt. How could people be so ungrateful?

I had no option but to reconcile, but the crew did not. They refused to take the news lying down. They anchored me at the entrance to the port, blocking all egress and ingress. About 1200 passengers had to be ferried to the shore. The striking crew's demand was that I should remain in service. But they added another demand–that their wages be enhanced by 35 per cent. This was one of the reasons, I suppose, that the protest did not succeed. I was anchored on 7th December, 1974 at a distant quay at *Le Havre* – the pier of the forgotten! I remained in that neglected condition for nearly four years. I came to know that a section of the French people was deeply disappointed with the treatment meted out to me and they did express it in different ways.

I become the *SS Norway* – a cruise liner

Can you understand the agony and pain of solitude? There was nobody to talk to, nobody to listen, nobody to look at except the engulfing darkness and the endless sea. I spent my days amidst the surging waves and the deep mysterious sounds that arose from the abysmal depths of the sea. Loneliness kills the soul. It drives one insane. I wanted to serve France – the country of my birth – till the end of my life. Even if I were incapacitated, I could still have been used as a museum or a hotel, with a few changes and repairs. I wanted to be with my people who loved me. But I was insulted, humiliated and abandoned. I was left with no option but to either perish at the pier, or serve some other master.

In 1977, Akram Ojjeh, a Saudi Arabian millionaire, proposed to use me as a floating museum. The Soviet Union disclosed plans to convert me into a hotel in the Black Sea. Even China came forward with the idea of using me as a floating industrial trade fair. But none of these proposals materialized. Finally, in 1979, Knut Kloster, the owner of the Norwegian Caribbean Line (NCL) purchased me for $18 million. I must concede that finally someone – though not from my own country – realized my worth. He had decided to convert me into the world's largest cruise ship.

In August 1979, I was taken to the Lloyd Werft Shipyard in Bremerhaven, Germany where an expensive renovation (costing approximately $80 million) was carried out. My name was also changed. I was registered now as the *SS Norway* in Oslo and was re-christened on 14th April, 1980 as the world's first super-liner. No one ever relishes a change of identity, a change of name and place. It washes off your past, makes you a stranger to yourself and offends dignity. But I had no option. I knew I was now destined to start my journey afresh – this time not as a nation's pride, but as an ordinary cruiser ferrying tourists on leisure voyages.

During the numerous tranquil nights, I had rested at sea, I had noted that waves, once they have passed, don't meet again. I would also not meet those waves again. The good old days were over. There was no point in being nostalgic. The past should not be allowed to determine the remaining course of one's life. I had overheard many wise conversations and had seen old people enthusiastic and eager to learn new things. I would try now to be like them—accept the changes demanded cheerfully and look forward instead to what the future had in store for me.

My first maiden voyage as the *SS Norway* was to Miami in 1980. Seeing the presence of an international crew, a departure was made from convention and the UN's flag was hoisted instead in the presence of King Olav V. I was supposed to travel passenger-less from Germany to Miami. But later on, a few select passengers joined this trip. From Oslo, I stopped at Southampton (England) and finally reached New York.

The inaugural seven-day cruise from Miami commenced on 1st June, 1980, with only two stoppages—the first at Little San Salvador (known as Great Stirrup Cay) and the second at St. Thomas US VI. This continued to be my schedule for a fairly long period. Later, Nassau (Bahamas) was also added to the trip. In 1985, St. Maarten and the Netherlands Antilles were also added. From 1987, my itinerary became a seven-day cruise starting from Miami and halting at St. Maarten, St. John, US VI, St. Thomas and Great Stirrup Cay. Much later, western Caribbean cruises were introduced with a seven days' journey, stopping at Cozumel, Mexico, Grand Cayman, Cayman Island, Rotan and Great Stirrup Cay. In between, I also cruised to the western Mediterranean, the western european coast, Northern Europe, the British Isles and the Norwegian fjords. Luckily, I turned out to be a popular cruise ship owing to my size, capacity and the air of grandeur which I carried. Many competitors started imitating me by using large ships as cruise vessels. As competition grew, in 1990, my owners decided to add two more decks with an additional 135 new suites and luxury cabins, to maintain my position as the "grand dame" of the Caribbean. There were some more fittings and alterations done to me to comply with the SOLAS (Safety of Life at Sea) Regulations in the years 1993 and 1996.

But in the world outside, changes were coming very fast. Inspite of the cruise trips doing quite well, the Norwegian Caribbean Line (NCL) started paying less attention to normal wear and tear issues. There was severe cutbacks to the repair regime resulting in mechanical breakdowns, fires, safety violations, etc. At times, there were also allegations of illegal waste dumping. When bad times come, everything goes wrong. Things happen over which you have no control. Maybe that is the meaning of destiny!

Sometime in 1999, as I was entering Barcelona on my way to Norway, fire erupted in the turbo-recharger. As a result, I was kept out of service for a few weeks. After repairs, I started on a major journey – probably my last – on 9th September, 2001, from Manhattan's west side pier for a transatlantic crossing to Greenock, Scotland and then Le Havre. Though NCL had made some cosmetic changes in order to put me back in circulation as a cruiser from Miami, the effort ultimately failed. As if in continuity, after I had docked at Miami on 25th May, 2003, another disaster occurred at 6.37 am. The boiler exploded. The disaster led to the death of eight crew members and seventeen critically injured. Though no passenger was hurt, the National Transportation Safety Board decided that the probable cause of the boiler's rupture could be sourced to the deficient operation, maintenance and inspection practices. Therefore, on 27th June, 2003, the NCL decided to relocate me to an unknown destination somewhere in Europe. I was finally taken to Bremerhaven on 23rd September, 2003. By then, NCL had already taken a decision to discard me altogether and therefore refused to repair the boiler, though it was easily repairable. At Bremerhaven, I was turned into accommodation for training NCL crews.

From *SS Norway*–the cruiser to *SS Blue Lady*–the scrap

Then came the bombshell.

On 23rd March, 2004, the NCL Chief Executive Colin Veitch declared: "The *Norway* will never sail again." The vessel's (mine) ownership was now transferred to Star Cruises, NCL's parent company. I was not allowed to leave Germany, owing to the existence of large amounts of asbestos embedded in different parts of the vessel. That is how ships were constructed then. I understand that the use of asbestos, to a great extent, is avoided nowadays. Another hurdle came in my way. My movement to any other country was now obstructed due to an international agreement called the Basel Convention.[30]

In these circumstances, Star Cruises appears to have successfully persuaded (actually misled) the German authorities into believing that I would go for repairs to Asia, and thereafter, for further cruise operations to Australia. It was from this point onwards that my story took a strange twist. I became the victim of a series of mis-representations and falsehoods. If the story of repair had not been concocted, I would have remained in Germany or somewhere in Europe as a relic of past glory. But on 10th August, 2005 I was betrayed and taken from Bremerhaven, allegedly "under tow" to Port Klang in Malaysia for the so-called 'repairs'. A deal, however, had already been struck, for in December of that year, it became apparent that I had been sold to an American naval demolition dealer for my scrap value – the actual demolition, however, to be done in India. As luck would have it, the falsehood was exposed by an environmental organization– Greenpeace – and other environmental activists. The exposure led to the cancellation of the deal. I was allowed to remain in Malaysia. But the scrap-dealers had widened their net and in January 2006, came the news of another deal. This time, I was sold by NCL to one Bridgend Shipping Limited of Monrovia, Liberia, for a consideration of $10 (in words, Ten United States Dollars)[A-1] as disclosed in the Bill of Sale entered at the Commonwealth of the Bahamas. Was it not a fake deal? How could the consideration be only ten dollars?

The problem was that I could not have been taken out from a Malaysian port as scrap due to the prohibition contained in the Basel Convention. The new buyer now created a new story that I was being taken to Dubai for repairs. This was a ruse. Instead of Dubai, I was taken to Bangladesh. The owner thought Bangladesh – being a third world country and in need of cheap steel – would allow my entry as scrap. But, in February 2006,[31(A-2)] Bangladesh refused entry on the ground that the ship contained huge amounts of asbestos and other hazardous substances onboard, and that it had not been decontaminated prior to its export, as per the Basel Convention.

With Bangladesh refusing entry, and after waiting for three weeks, I was taken towards India's territorial waters on 5th May, 2006. The Malaysian Government in a letter dated 19th May, 2006[A-3] addressed to the Consumers Association of Penang, had claimed that the *SS Norway* had left Malaysian waters for Dubai, for repairs. I have no idea when Haryana Ship Demolition Pvt. Ltd., (operating as Regent Shipping) purchased me from Bridgend Shipping Limited, which is when I got my present name – *Blue Lady*! While I was anchored in Malaysia, it was officially claimed that the ship had been scrapped and that it could not travel. The veracity of this claim was highly disputed. I sometimes wonder whether destiny is ever your own creation or whether you are driven helplessly in its direction by others!

***Blue Lady* at Alang, India, awaiting scrapping**

Story of The *Blue Lady*

Destiny

From now onwards, we start the story of the *Blue Lady*. The name, as I told you at the beginning, intrigued everyone. Compared to the lives of the *SS France* and even the *SS Norway*, mine is a sad story of insult, greed and deceit. I know Sir, I have taken a considerable part of your precious time. But may I please request you to bear with me for some more time? I am sure you are curious to know what brought me to the present impasse. I will make an effort to tell you everything that I heard and saw till my last breath, including the details of the legal battle of which I became a part. The events that I have narrated to you so far had already prepared me physically and mentally for the worst. But there were yet so many things that I was destined to see, none of them, I would say, belonged any longer to the realm of the good. Is life like that?

Another request, hope you wouldn't mind if while narrating my story, I refer myself in third person, as a ship or a vessel, occasionally, that will also avoid too much of "I".

I arrive in India – the legal battle ensues

India, rated as a developing country, was facing the problem of dumping of all kinds of wastes, including hazardous wastes, by the industrialized countries. I knew about India during the days of my sea voyages. I had seen Indian people, heard their conversations both superficial and deep. I had come to the conclusion that human beings are the same everywhere except for their individual traditions and culture; traits like greed, envy, jealousy and comparison are common everywhere. But I was keen to know more. I, therefore, gathered many facts and information while I was anchored off the Malaysian coast and even thereafter.

I came to know that prior to my arrival, legal proceedings were already pending in the Supreme Court of India, where a High Powered Committee headed by one Prof. M.G.K Menon, a scientist, had been appointed.[32] These proceedings were initiated in the public interest to bring a halt to the dumping of toxic and other wastes by the developed countries and to enforce the Basel Convention which India had signed and ratified, and was therefore bound by its international commitments. The Menon Committee made several recommendations on how the dumping of toxic wastes from outside countries could be checked. It also looked into how hazardous wastes generated within India were required to be handled. I am not concerned about these other issues except the activity of shipbreaking. Sending ships to India for breaking up for scrap was considered by the Menon Committee as a part of the dumping of toxic wastes by the developed countries.[33]

The Committee's report showed how the ship-breaking activity was being conducted off the sea coast at Alang,[34] with utter disregard for the environment and health of the workers involved. The Committee was of the view that developed countries – after their ships became unusable and had been reduced to a mere "floating waste" – knowingly allowed them to be despatched to the developing/under-developed countries which accepted them due to poverty, the availability of cheap labour, lack of strict regulations and their implementation, as well as general apathy towards the environment. This was against the letter and spirit of the provisions of the Basel Convention.

Earlier generation ships used asbestos as a filling material for insulation. This was done due to unawareness about its harm to the environment and human health. I belonged to that generation of ships containing substantial amounts of asbestos. Asbestos was embedded in my structure. There were also other substances which were not environmentally benign, like PCBs.

A significant verdict was handed down by the Supreme Court of India in these proceedings on 14th October, 2003.[35 (A-11)] The court ruled that international commitments under the Basel Convention are binding and can be read into the municipal law. The country exporting hazardous waste must ensure that the country of import has all the facilities to deal with the said waste in an environmentally sound manner.

I don't wish to explain the judgment like a lawyer, but I would like to set out what was important from the point of view of deciding my fate. The court said that prior to arrival in India, a ship must have a declaration from the exporting country which stated that the ship did not contain any hazardous or radioactive substances and that it would be properly decontaminated by its owner before it was dispatched for dismantling. Decontamination of the ship prior to its export was thus an important condition. A Monitoring Committee was also appointed by the court to oversee the implementation of its judgment.

I will tell you a little later how I eventually entered India's territorial waters. For, at this juncture, and before I proceed any further, I must recount to you another shipbreaking-related incident that occurred (in February 2006) just three months prior to my arrival; it will make my story clearer. A French warship named the *Clemenceau* was allowed by the French Government to leave for India without prior decontamination. It carried asbestos, PCB and other toxic substances. In an extraordinary response to international pressures and protests, the French Government decided to recall the vessel. The Indian Supreme Court acknowledged this in its order passed on 17th February, 2006. However, the Court also constituted a Committee of Technical Experts to evolve guidelines for ship-breaking for future contingencies and to assess the capacity and infrastructure available for such activities at Alang (Gujarat)–the famous ship-breaking yard of India.

PART-IV

The Story of SS *Clemenceau*

The mighty aircraft carrier

I did not know why I was being taken towards India's territorial waters, when everyone in the world was already aware of the fate of the *Clemenceau*.

I had heard the story of the *Clemenceau* from the Captain and the crew members. From my earlier voyages, and from what people said, I had come to know that the *Clemenceau* had been named after Georges Benjamin Clemenceau, another French President. I have already highlighted the passion France had for passenger liners, but after the Second World War, it also became crazy and excited to build aircraft carriers. As usual, France wanted its aircraft carrier to be an object of national pride. It was quite eager to replace British and American war carriers.

Let me enlighten you that there was not much of a time gap between the birth of the *Clemenceau* and myself. The *Clemenceau*'s construction – with the nickname '*Le Clem*' – was initiated at the port of St. Nazaire and finally completed at the Brest Shipyard, France. The keel was laid in November 1955 and the carrier was launched on 21st December, 1957. However, the formal commissioning took place only on 22nd November, 1961. If you will recall, I was launched on 11th May, 1960.

The *Clemenceau* was an 869 feet long aircraft carrier, with a deck so designed that it could allow the simultaneous launch of multiple aircrafts. It could carry up to forty combat war-planes, heavy gun armaments, and nuclear munitions. It was later on also equipped to fire nuclear missiles.

The *Clemenceau* was the sixth aircraft carrier of the French Navy, which participated during the Cold War with such changes as were required. It was quite handsome and sturdy, and displayed masculine characteristics. I would therefore prefer to refer to the *Clemenceau* as 'he', though all ships, by convention, are addressed as 'she'! After all, at this moment, I am only a story-teller. Let me disclose at the outset that the *Clemenceau* travelled more than one million nautical miles, which, in fact, would mean, it circumnavigated the globe 48 times! During its active period (from 1961 to 1997), the aircraft carrier spent 3125 days at sea and executed more than 70,000 catapult-launches.

The *Clemenceau* participated in a majority of the naval operations carried out by France. These operations invariably carried secret names. *Big Game* was the operation carried out in the western Mediterranean as an anti-submarine aircraft carrier, together with NATO and the US Sixth Fleet from 12th January - 5th February, 1962. Another NATO exercise in the Gibraltar Zone called *OTAN Dawn Breeze VII* was conducted from 9th March to 2nd April,1962. In January 1968, the *Clemenceau* was involved in the search of the *Minerve,* a submarine reported lost in the Mediterranean. The *Clemenceau* also participated in the testing of the first French hydrogen bomb at Polynesia the same year (1968). Two important operations – *Saphire-I* and *Saphire-II* – were carried out during 1974-77 in support of Djibouti, by deploying the *Clemenceau* off the African coast in the Indian Ocean. In 1983-84, the *Clemenceau* found itself deployed in the east Mediterranean during the Lebanese civil war. During 1987-88, *Clemenceau* was placed in the Gulf of Oman in the war between Iraq and Iran under *Operation Prometheus*. In other well-known operations, *Desert Shield* and *Desert Storm*, the *Clemenceau* along with the cruiser *Colbert* and tanker *Var*, helped transport 40 helicopters, among other equipment. As a part

SS Clemenceau – the mighty aircraft carrier

of the coalition, the *Clemenceau* participated in the Gulf War to defeat Saddam Hussein in 1991, after Iraq had invaded Kuwait in 1990. Between 1993 to 1996, the *Clemenceau* carried out *Operation Balbuzard*, as part of combat operations and patrolling over former Yugoslavia in support of the UN Forces and thereafter, *Operation Salamandre* in the Adriatic Sea during the Yugoslav conflict. But besides being engaged in battles and warfare, the *Clemenceau* also acted as host to several fine artists for days, weeks and months. The aircraft carrier was decommissioned on 1st October, 1997.

Another sad story

What is important, however, is what happened to this illustrious ship thereafter.

France initially thought of scrapping the *Clemenceau* at its own Naval Shipyard but found the exercise prohibitively expensive. Therefore, the *Clemenceau* had to suffer the humiliation of being taken from one place to another to be scrapped. From 1997 to 2001, some parts of the carrier were sold to the Brazilian Government, which owned the *MV Foch* – another aircraft carrier, later renamed the *MV Sao Paulo*. At some point, there was a proposal to sink the *Clemenceau* in the middle of the ocean so that it could be used as a life-like target during high-sea military exercises. This was, however, opposed and rightly so. The silly idea was finally dropped. Another proposal came from the City of Marseille in 2001, to sink the aircraft carrier in the Mediterranean Sea to create an 'artificial reef'. This plan remained 'under consideration' till 2003 but was finally abandoned. Many such wild ideas kept emerging in creative French minds, but the French Government was only too keen to get rid of its liability as soon as possible.

It was, therefore, decided to sell the ship in a public auction on the condition that the decontamination (of asbestos mainly) would take place in Europe and that till the completion of this exercise, France would be its registered owner. A Spanish company – Gijonesa – won the auction. They wanted to take it to Spain but Spain refused its entry. The company therefore decided to take it to Turkey. But Turkey also refused on the ground that it would constitute an illegal trade. The *Clemenceau* thus remained stranded in the mid-Mediterranean sea. For non-fulfilment of conditions, the contract with the Spanish company was terminated.

The next highest bidder was the Ship Decommissioning Industries Company (SDIC) and Eckhardt Marine Gmbh, both from Hamburg, Germany.

The contract between SDIC and the French Government was signed on 20th October, 2003 with the condition that the decontamination of the 'hull' would take place in Greece and thereafter, it would be taken to India for demolition. Greece declined to allow decontamination resulting in cancellation of the contract. The *Clemenceau* was brought back to Toulon, France. The SDIC then signed a new contract with the French Government on 23rd June, 2004. A sub-contract was also entered into between SDIC and Technopure for decontaminating the ship at Toulon itself.

At this point came the controversial announcement by the French Ministry of Defence that Technopure would remove 95% of the asbestos and that only 22 tons of asbestos would remain for removal in India. For this purpose, Technopure would train the concerned technicians in India. It appears that Technopure did not complete its job satisfactorily and therefore, another agency 'Prestosid' was engaged in asbestos removal. The *Clemenceau* finally left the Toulon military base of France on the 31st December, 2005 for demolition at Alang, India. There was severe criticism globally, public protests were held and legal actions were initiated. The ship did not have a complete inventory of asbestos waste, PCBs and other toxic substances and the claims of the French authorities were found to be misleading.

Coincidentally, it was around this same period that Star Cruises had misled the German authorities with the news that I was being taken to Asia for repairs–an outright lie. The plan was to take me out of the jurisdiction of Europe for dismantling without decontamination, which the Basel Convention, among others, did not permit. In December 2005, I was at Port Klang, Malaysia when the *Clemenceau* was on its way towards India.

The recall

In the meanwhile, in India, as I have already told you, the Supreme Court had delivered a verdict (14th October, 2003) and a committee had been constituted to ensure the implementation of the various directions given in the judgment. This committee – called as the Supreme Court Monitoring Committee (SCMC) – started receiving complaints from January 2005 itself about *Clemenceau's* imminent arrival in India. The SCMC had expressed its view (in February 2005) that the *Clemenceau* – admittedly carrying asbestos waste – would not be allowed entry in India. After the *Clemenceau's* journey towards India was announced in December 2005, the SCMC met again (in January 2006) and decided that the *Clemenceau* should not be allowed within the Exclusive Economic Zone (EEZ) of the country. Thereafter, the SCMC held a crucial meeting on 20th January, 2006 at which the French Government and other stakeholders were present. The French Government had also filed an affidavit dated 19th January, 2006, in which it took the position that ships are not a hazardous waste under the Basel Convention and that decontamination of the hull had already taken place in France prior to its departure. The affidavit also claimed that only a balance of 45 tonnes of asbestos/ asbestos-containing material was left for decontamination at Alang.

After hearing all stake-holders, the SCMC submitted a split report to the Supreme Court on 6th February, 2006. Some members (the majority) accepted the representation of the French Government that the *Clemenceau* was left with only 45 MT of asbestos and that in the absence of any inventory regarding the presence of PCBs, the ship as a whole could not be said to be a hazardous waste. Other members (the minority) did their own detailed study and came to the conclusion that France continued to be the owner of the *Clemenceau* and therefore, was fully responsible for the consequences. The minority report referred to the Basel Convention and questioned how the *Clemenceau* could have been allowed to leave Toulon (France) without a detailed inventory of the hazardous wastes on board. Referring to data contained in several documents, it refused to accept the stand of the French Government that 115 tons of asbestos had already been removed from the ship and that there were no PCBs on board. The Committee also noticed the presence of some radioactive material. These minority members of SCMC recommended that the Indian Government should take appropriate steps to ensure that the *Clemenceau* "does not ever enter India or its sovereign waters."

The Supreme Court had already accepted (on 16th January, 2006), the undertaking of the SDIC that the *Clemenceau* would not enter the Exclusive Economic Zone (EEZ) until the next date of hearing.[36] When the SCMC's split verdict was placed before the court (on 13th February, 2006), it decided instead to appoint another team of experts.[37] Though the *Clemenceau* was still not permitted to enter the EEZ, the Court permitted the importer of the ship to file the Bill of Entry with the customs authorities. Shockingly, the court also saw fit to pass a gag order, restraining the media from reporting further about the ship. This gag order drew international criticism and, I think, rightly so. On what grounds could anybody be restrained from commenting on a ship that was found sailing in violation of laws?

Meanwhile, a legal action was initiated by a few French NGOs before a French Civil Court in Paris. The French court declined to entertain the plea on the ground that the *Clemenceau* contained war-related material and therefore, it lacked the jurisdiction to adjudicate the issue. The matter was then taken to the Administrative Tribunal on appeal, but the Tribunal too refused the NGOs' claims. Finally, the issue was placed before the *Conseil d'Etat* (The French Supreme Court) which suspended the decision to send the decommissioned carrier to India for scrapping. Pursuant to this order, plus world-wide criticism and international pressures, Jacques Chirac, President of France, decided on 15th February, 2006 to recall the *Clemenceau.* When the issue came up again before the Indian Supreme Court on 17th February, 2006, it merely noted the decision of the French Government and did not pursue the matter any further. I know only this much. I have no idea about what eventually happened with the *Clemenceau* and where it was taken for dismantling.[38]

PART-V: My Final Days

The precedent set in the case of the *Clemenceau* ought to have been followed in mine as well. But that did not happen and this quite surprised me. If that course had been adopted, I would not have been at Alang, India. My destiny would have been quite different. Perhaps I would not have been even telling you this story. So, how did my destiny change again? Who was responsible? I will try to explain it all to you in a very simple language, although we are steadily venturing into the realm of law.

I appreciate your patience, my friend. I assure you I will not be too subjective. Before I proceed further, let me candidly confess that my knowledge of law is limited only to what I have heard during conversations. However, my varied experience has added immensely to my common sense about things. I think that makes analysis easier. One can at least decipher what is right and what is wrong. These are legal issues and I cannot afford to be inaccurate in my narration. Someone may accuse me of contempt of court, even when I am no longer alive!

The departure from the precedent set for the *Clemenceau* led to an environmental activist petitioning the Supreme Court that the *Blue Lady* should not be allowed to enter India's territorial waters as this would be in violation of the Basel Convention and the Court's order of 13th October, 2003. The petition alleged that the ship contained 1250 tonnes of asbestos waste, PCBs, mercury, low-level radioactive substances, hazardous chemicals, etc.[39]

The court took note of this petition and on 12th May, 2006 directed the Technical Expert Committee (TEC) – already examining these very issues – to examine this complaint as well.[40] Significantly, the Ministry of Environment and Forests acted swiftly and directed the Gujarat Pollution Control Board on the following day itself (13th May), not to permit the ship [me] into the country's territorial waters till the issue was decided by the TEC. This direction was simply reiterated by the Gujarat Pollution Control Board to my owners.

Immediately thereafter, through a letter dispatched on 15th May itself, a new party calling itself the Haryana Ship Demolition Pvt Ltd, claimed that it was the "bonafide purchaser" of the ship from M/s Bridgend Shipping Ltd.[41] The party also offered a self-assessment of the substances on the vessel, submitting that it contained "1240 MT of ACM, 85% of it as partition walls and ceilings of rooms." The letter also made an appeal on humanitarian grounds: "*There are 13 crew members on board "Blue Lady" with limited amount of fuel, fresh water and provisions for their survival. The currents in high seas in this part of the ocean are very strong, especially when the monsoon is setting in. Therefore, it will not be a safe location to anchor the ship, as the current may break the anchor and the ship may start drifting.*" It also made a commitment: "*In case the Committee decides not to allow the ship for breaking at Alang, we hereby undertake to tow the ship away into territorial waters, which can be done with ease.*" Two days thereafter (on 17th May) Haryana Ship Demolition Pvt Ltd., made a *volte face*. It now claimed that the *Blue Lady* was a "dead ship" and should be allowed to enter Indian sovereign jurisdiction for beaching as the weather conditions were getting worse.

These were gross misrepresentations. Who would know better than me? When I was taken out from the Malaysian port of Klang, it was on the excuse that I was being taken to Dubai for repairs, where was the need to seek anchorage in Indian territorial waters? There was documentary proof of these facts.[42 (A-3)] I am amazed how humans can utter such brazen lies in their courts. How could they declare me "dead" when I was very much alive? Maybe I was tired, worn out or, greatly lacking the enthusiasm of my younger days. All that might be there. But in no uncertain terms could I have been considered a dead ship!

Interim Report of the Technical Expert Committee (TEC)

The Technical Experts Committee submitted its interim report on the *Blue Lady* to the Supreme Court on 20th May, 2006.[43] The interim report specifically recorded the statement of the owner – Haryana Ship Demolition Pvt Ltd – in the following words: "*As the ship cannot be safely anchored in the high sea, the cost of holding the ship with two tugs would be in the range of USD 30,000 for the day.*" Therefore, the company requested that anchorage of the ship in the Indian territorial waters at Alang may be permitted. The ship owner's undertaking was also recorded: "*In case it is not finally permitted to break the ship at Alang, they would tow their ship away into international waters, which can be done with ease.*" The Gujarat Enviro Protection and Infrastructure

Limited (GEPIL) also filed an affidavit in which it claimed that out of 1240 MT of asbestos, 1050 MT contained in the walls and ceiling panels would be reusable. It also claimed that it would not be technically feasible to quantify the PCB contents in cables, paints, flooring, etc.

On the basis of this alleged representation from the owner – M/S Haryana Ship Demolition Pvt Ltd – the TEC was misled in proceeding to recommend permission for anchoring the ship in India's territorial waters. It accepted the specious plea that the monsoon was likely to set in shortly, leading to rough conditions in the high seas and that the provisions on board for the sparse crew were limited. As far as beaching of the ship was concerned, the committee itself noted that beaching was irreversible and therefore, during the period, the ship would remain anchored. The Gujarat Pollution Control Board would undertake verification of all hazardous materials on board while the ship is anchored and beaching permission may not be given if the vessel were found to contain any hazardous substances of any kind or quantity "which cannot be safely removed, handled and disposed off at Alang." The TEC made it clear that permission for dismantling of the ship would only be considered subsequently on the basis of a decommissioning plan to be submitted by M/s Haryana Ship Demolition Pvt. Ltd.

On 30th May, 2006, the Technical Expert Committee itself moved an unprecedented application before the Supreme Court seeking permission to anchor the *Blue Lady*[44] in the Indian territorial waters. The stand taken by the TEC was opposed by the environmental groups on the ground that the entry of the *Blue Lady* in Indian territorial waters would be in blatant violation of the Supreme Court's judgment of 14th October, 2003 by which the court had specifically directed that without "prior decontamination" no ship could be permitted to enter the country's waters.[45]

In their support, the environmental groups relied heavily on an order passed by the Bangladesh authorities on 5th February, 2006 which categorically rejected entry of the ship into Bangladesh by relying upon the Basel Convention's provisions. The environmentalists also referred to the letter dated 19th May, 2006 of the Malaysian authorities, which had noted that the *SS Norway* had left Malaysian waters for Dubai on 5th May, 2006 at 03:00 PM for "repair works." They reminded the court that instead, the ship was illegally diverted towards the Indian territorial waters for dismantling and that such misleading information amounted to indulging in illegal traffic. They also argued that following the tradition set by the French Government regarding the *Clemenceau,* the Malaysian Government should recall the *Blue Lady*.

The report submitted by the Technical Experts Committee was strange, to say the least. It defied simple logic as to how a ship which was shown on official records as going to Dubai for repairs could be diverted to another country for dismantling as scrap without that country's express prior permission and knowledge and without knowing what hazardous substances the ship contained. The fact that the ship contained hazardous waste was known to everybody. The TEC knew very well that the reason I was disallowed from leaving Bremerhaven earlier was the quantity of hazardous waste packed in my structure.

All these wrong and misleading statements constituting violation of law ought to have prompted the Supreme Court to decline the request for anchoring me in Indian waters. But sadly, the court also did not heed the logic. On the basis of TEC's interim report, the court, on 5th June 2006, ordered action be taken in terms of the recommendations of the report "but this would not confer any equity in favour of the owner of the ship."[46] This paved the way for the Ministry of Environment and Forests to issue permission on 10th June for anchoring the ship "off Alang Port."[47]

Violation of Supreme Court Order: the *Blue Lady moves* to Dubai

Even as this was happening, even stranger developments were in store. Contrary to what the ship's owner had represented before the court, instead of the ship being anchored "off-Alang" in the Indian waters, it was turned round and "towed" to the UAE! It was docked at Fujairah (UAE) for two days.[48] Thereafter, it was towed back to the edge of Indian waters and anchored 35 nautical miles from Alang at Pipavav port, also in Gujarat. I heard that a prominent newspaper – the *Khaleej Times* had reported on 30th June, 2006 that as per the order passed by the Supreme Court, the *Blue Lady* was due to anchor at Alang at 8.40 am on Friday, but instead, it was towed to the UAE.[49 (A-5)] Thus, entirely misleading and incorrect information was given by the owners of the ship to the government as well as to the Supreme Court of India. These facts proved that the pleas and requests made in the letters by the owners–Haryana Ship Demolition Pvt Ltd – were all an eye wash, in fact, brazen falsehoods. While observing these events with amusement, I kept asking myself, "Is the law really blind?"

I heard that apparently during this brief period, a new proposal was being made under the rubric of "Project Dubai." It was conceived in order to rescue the *Blue Lady* from demolition. A joint UAE/US consortium of investors was willing to make an expenditure of $120 million to refurbish and bring the ship to Dubai to serve as a floating hotel for conferences, restaurant and as a cultural centre. The US partner of Project Dubai wanted to remove the asbestos in a safe manner after it was brought back to Dubai. The UAE partner also commented that the ship was still beautiful – a work of art. "She needs cleaning and some attention," he said, and added that it could become the kind of niche project envisioned by HH Sheikh Mohammad bin Rashid al Maktaum to bring the cultures of other nations into Dubai.[50] Hearing this news made me happy that there were still people who recognized my worth and didn't treat me as waste, an expression I had by now come increasingly to detest. The news generated a faint hope in me.

On 23rd September, 2006, *Tehelka News*[A-7] released an important statement made on the basis of a naval intelligence report generated in late 2004.[51 (A-8)] Apparently, the naval report had expressed apprehensions surrounding the unchecked movements of vessels like the *Blue Lady* and the *Clemenceau* which allowed them to carry contraband, bombs, etc. The report, in fact, clearly mentioned that some ships which arrive at Alang for dismantling disappear from anchorage after a short while to unknown destinations. The report apprehended that there was likelihood of ships being involved in undesirable activities and went on to allege the involvement of Pakistani nationals represented by the Dawood gang.

In this context, I may emphasise that it still remains a mystery, why the *Blue Lady* was towed to Dubai when its owners had represented to the Indian Government as well as to the Supreme Court that the ship needed to be anchored in Indian waters on humanitarian grounds and had even provided an undertaking! Though these facts were brought to the notice of the Indian Government as well as the Supreme Court, unfortunately, no serious note was taken of them; no investigation or inquiry was ordered, not to speak of passing an adverse order.

A namesake inspection

The Gujarat Pollution Control Board (GPCB) sent a team in July 2006 for a pre-inspection of the *Blue Lady*. The actual inspection was carried out on 11th-12th July, 2006. There was no inventory of hazardous wastes made by the Malaysian authorities which the team could use to compare while carrying out the inspection. The investigation turned out to be an eyewash. The inspection team recorded as its conclusion: "The team did not observe any hazardous material in loose form on board except oil rags." As regards quantification of PCBs, it estimated without any basis that this would be less than 10 MT. Finally it opined that safe removal, handling and disposal of asbestos, ACMs, PCBs and other hazardous wastes could be done at Alang. The report of the GPCB was considered and approved by the Technical Expert Committee on 29th July 2006, in spite of all the legal violations.

It is in these rather strange conditions that the *Blue Lady* was finally cleared for beaching. I had no option but to watch these events helplessly.

Irreversible beaching

Surprisingly, on 31st July, 2006, M/s Priya Blue Industries Pvt. Ltd., a completely new actor, put up a letter to claim that it was the "new buyer" of the vessel.[52] All previous correspondence for granting permission to anchor, beach and dismantle had been sought by M/s Haryana Ship Demolition Pvt. Ltd., which all of a sudden disappeared from the scene. The *Business Standard*, a financial daily, put out a report that the Haryana Ship Demolition Ltd. had sold the vessel to Priya Blue Shipping Ltd. for $16 million. Look at the difference between this sale and the earlier sale, which was for only ten US dollars!

On 1st August, 2006, a Deputy Director in the Ministry of Environment and Forest (MoEF), Government of India, issued an unprecedented communication to the Gujarat Maritime Board to proceed further with the matter of issuing beaching permission to the owners of the *Blue Lady.*[53] The Gujarat Maritime Board duly obliged and issued the beaching permission within two days (on 3rd August, 2006). The beaching permission was granted without the court's permission.

With the beaching permit in hand, the *Blue Lady* was finally beached (on 15th August, 2006) at Alang approximately 4000 feet away from the shore.[54] The act of beaching cleared all hurdles for the ship's dismantling. In November 2006, M/s Priya Blue Industries Pvt. Ltd. moved an application seeking permission for lightening and dismantling the structure.[55] This was vehemently opposed by the environmentalists who enlisted in their cause a series of violations and misleading statements made before the Supreme Court.[56] Prof. M.G.K. Menon – earlier Chairperson of the High Powered Committee on Hazardous Wastes that had submitted a comprehensive report on ship-breaking and which became the basis of the court's judgment of 14th October, 2003 also now decided to join the issue. On 14th August, 2006, he addressed a letter to the then Chief Justice of the Supreme Court advising against beaching of the ship.[57 (A-6)] Professor Menon reminded the court that the *Blue Lady* belonged to Star Cruises and it was their responsibility and that of the Government of Malaysia to ensure that the ship was either reconditioned as a maritime liner or to ensure its disposal in an environmentally sound manner – as had been done by the French Government in the case of the *Clemenceau*. He cited the court's order of 14th October, 2003 and said that any effort to dilute the concept of prior decontamination would be a measure going against the interest of the workers in the shipbreaking yards and also a violation of the Basel Convention, both by Malaysia and India, who were signatories to the Convention. He made it clear that the only option, even if beaching were done, was to return the *Blue Lady* to Malaysia.

But none of these persuasions and sane counsel really worked!

Dismantling

The TEC had submitted its final report on 30th August, 2006, regarding the shipbreaking and the health of the workers. Meanwhile, on 4th December, 2006, the Supreme Court passed an interim order directing the Gujarat Pollution Control Board to take an appropriate decision on the dismantling plan submitted by M/s Priya Blue Industries Ltd.[58] Pursuant thereto, the Gujarat Pollution Control Board constituted a committee to examine the dismantling plan. The committee sought an opinion from the Gujarat Maritime Board. On 1st January, 2007, the Board wrote to say that "since the vessel has been beached by tug power she has moved onto the shore with full force and thus has settled deep into the shore with a likelihood of bottom damage." Therefore, the Board wrote, it would not be possible to pull back the vessel after it had been beached. On the basis of this opinion, the committee also came to the conclusion that there was no scope for sending back the *Blue Lady* after it had been permitted to be beached. The committee also accepted the dismantling plan, with a few conditions.

The environmentalists again opposed the view taken by the GPCB and filed an affidavit on 24th Feb, 2007. Besides pointing out the violation of the court's order of 14th October, 2003 as well as provisions of the Basel Convention, environmental groups drew attention to the affidavit filed on 2nd June, 2006 by the MoEF itself before the court, in which the MOEF had taken a clear position with regard to prior decontamination: "I submit that India has consistently taken a stand that ships prior to dismantling should be decontaminated to the extent possible." Another fact which was added to the list of misleading statements made by M/s Haryana Ship Demolition Pvt. Ltd.

was that on 19th January, 2006, the *Blue Lady* (then, *SS Norway*) had been sold by the Norwegian Cruise Line Ltd., while under the jurisdiction of the Commonwealth of Bahamas for consideration of a sum of $10 to Bridgend Shipping Ltd.

In the interim report of the Technical Expert Committee dated 20.05.2006, M/s Haryana Ships Demolition Pvt. Ltd. was allowed to participate in the proceedings on the basis of the claim that it had purchased the ship from M/s Brigend, but no document was ever submitted in support of this claim.

Back to the Technical Expert Committee (TEC)

On 12th March, 2007, the Supreme Court expressed the view that a further report from the Technical Expert Committee was required to see whether all conditions had been met before any action was taken on the dismantling plan.[59] The court said in its order that the question relating to "reversibility or impermissibility of the beaching" would be taken up after submission of the report. The TEC submitted its report on 10th May, 2007.[60] This report finally declared that the beaching was an irreversible process. Though the beaching permission was issued in violation of all existing legal provisions as well as directions of the court, a fresh position was now taken by the MoEF in its affidavit filed on 11th May, 2007 through one M. Subbarao. It now claimed that the beaching permission given to the ship *Blue Lady* was not in violation of the court's judgment dated 14th October, 2003. The affidavit went on to claim that the Basel Convention did not apply to vessels intended for recycling and that such vessels were not considered as hazardous wastes. A strongly objectionable statement was made in the affidavit in connection with the term 'decontamination': the MOEF now held that the term "decontamination" meant removal of hazardous wastes contained as cargo, and did not include (hazardous) materials embedded in the structure of the vessel.

I found this argument very strange. Who would carry asbestos waste as cargo? It was always embedded in the ships. It had always been understood that the hazardous wastes from shipbreaking became available once the ship was dismantled. It is for this reason that an assessment was required to be done in advance so that the waste so generated upon dismantling would be disposed of in an environmentally safe manner.

On 6th August, 2007, despite the TEC's report which categorically informed the court that beaching had already taken place, and despite the recycling and dismantling plan being flawed, the Supreme Court decided to accept the report's recommendations.

Presence of radioactive material and further inspections

The exercise carried out by the Technical Expert Committee was faulty. This was exposed by one Tom Haugen in a letter he addressed to the TEC on 19th July, 2007.[61 (A-9)] Haugen had been the project manager for engineering, delivery, installation, commissioning and upgrading of the fire detection system of the *Blue Lady* in 1990. In the letter he pointed out that there were new fire detection systems installed that had approximately 5500 detection points, each having 1100 radioactive element Americium 241. He warned that the removal of Americium 241 had to be done by skilled persons and all detectors used had to be destroyed in a safe way. The casual way in which the TEC had acted was further clear from the fact that in its 2006 report, it had said that there were no radioactive substances on the ship, in spite of a dissenting note from one of its members, Dr. Virendra Mishra of the Industrial Toxicology Research Centre, Lucknow. Dr Mishra had clearly stated that the "Presence of radioactive materials should be ascertained well in advance. Though it is mentioned in the report that radioactive material is not available, in my opinion, there is a possibility of the presence of radioactive materials due to the existence of liquid level indicators and smoke detectors on the ship." This important revelation made in the interest of public safety and health prompted the court to direct further inspection of the ship by the Atomic Energy Regulatory Board (AERB) and the Gujarat Maritime Board. After the inspection was carried out (on 14th August, 2007), they reported that they could find only 12 smoke detectors containing Americium 241.[62 (A-10)] These were handed over to the ship-breaker Priya Blue for disposal under the supervision of the AERB. The team concluded that the ship "now does not contain any radioactive material on board." Thus, 1088 smoke detectors having potential radioactive substances were left on the ship.

I am sure these radioactive substance would have reached the market, as most materials recovered from broken ships are sold for second-hand use at Alang itself.

Final orders of the Supreme Court

On 6th September, 2007, the Supreme Court passed an order reaffirming the directions it had given in its order dated 14th October, 2003.[63] However, the argument that prior decontamination of ships – namely, that before leaving the port of a foreign country for scrapping, a certificate that the ship was totally decontaminated should be obtained in consonance with the Basel Convention; was not accepted. The said convention as well as earlier directions given by the court were substantially diluted by holding that: "The authorities in India can, without the certificate at the stage of anchorage, verify and come to a conclusion that if the ship is contaminated, the same is to be sent back." This reasoning was seriously flawed and was decidedly against the interests of the workers and the environment.

On 11th September, 2007, the court passed another order accepting the dismantling and recycling plan submitted by M/s Priya Blue Industries Pvt. Ltd.[64] [(A-12)] The order acknowledged that the allegation made by the environmentalists concerning the presence of radioactive material on board the vessel was correct, but the court still relied upon the report prepared by the AERB. It did not consider the fact that as many as 1088 smoke detectors containing radioactive material were not traced by the AERB. Regarding asbestos containing material (ACM), which comprised 85% of the hazardous wastes from the ship, the court said that it was recyclable and could be sold in the market. Regarding the presence of PCBs, no determination was made except to say that the PCBs could either be disposed of in a land-fill or through incineration.

There was international condemnation of the report submitted by the Technical Expert Committee. It was said that the report was given under undue pressure to allow the ship to be beached; that the Committee had failed to follow the Basel Convention and the Supreme Court's order dated 14.10.2003 which held that ships must be decontaminated of hazardous waste substances such as PCBs and asbestos, and that there must be a full inventory of the hazardous substances which must be formally notified prior to arrival in the importing country. No such notification was made either by Malaysia (the last country of departure) or by Germany.

Adieu, my friend!

My last memories confirm that in spite of my beaching, I was fully afloat at high tide. The photos, artworks, furniture, including the murals in the windward dining room and children's playroom and the Steinway piano located in *Le Bistro* were still very much present on board. My admirers were concerned about the art pieces. For this reason, in early September 2006, the owner entered into agreements with various buyers, auctioneers and French museums to sell the artworks. During this time, when everybody was busy in pursuing their selfish interests, there were only a few people in France who still remembered me. One of them – Jean Philippe Prieur – spokesperson of the French Liner Association, said: "*SS France* is part of France's heritage." He added: "For a French person, scrapping *Le France* is like dismantling the Tower of London for a Briton." After I heard the final pronouncement of the Supreme Court handed down on 11th September, 2007, I looked at the vast sea and surging waves on which I had floated like a queen for numerous years. Now the end was at hand. The death warrant arrived in December, 2007 when it was confirmed that work on cutting the tip of the *Blue Lady's* bow would commence[65]– a ceremonial move done to most of the ships that end up at Alang before their full-scale breaking.

My story therefore ends here. Let me not add anything now. In silent contemplation looking at my eternal companion – the sea – let me perish. My stories will never die. I will remain alive in the hearts of those who loved me. Those who travelled with me would pass on their remembrances and souvenirs to the next generation. People would look for me in museums, in pictures and in books. Even when I take my last breath, I cannot detach myself from the sea on whose waves I grew up and saw this world. I feel as if the immortal sea is inviting me and I will be going to eternal sleep in its bosom!

Thanks, my friend, for giving me your company for so long as a patient listener. I hope you will narrate this 'tale of a ship' with the same passion with which you heard it from me. The words sung by Michel Sardou reverberate around me:

Don't ever call me *France* again,
France has just left me in the lurch
Don't ever call me *France* again,
This is my last will.
Adieu!

[By 12th July, 2008, the bow and the stern of the Blue Lady were removed and by September, most of the sections of the ship that remain above the water line had been cut and removed. The ship was completely broken by late 2008. In February, 2009, the tip of the bow of the Blue Lady's –"nose" – was brought back to France, the country

The bow on display in *Le Havre,* 2018

of her birth. It was put on public display at the Paris Yacht Marina, Port de Grenelle, Paris 15e. The two sets of neon letters which spell "France" were displayed at the Musee National de la Marina in Paris and were then sent to Le Havre and presented to the Musee Malraux, facing the front of the harbour. One Dick Jones, one time merchant mariner, wrote: "Ships are like life; there is a beginning and an end." Only memories remain.]

References

SS Normandie

1. James Hinton, *The Sinking of The S.S. Normandie at NYC's Pier 88,* New York History Blog (September 23, 2014), https://newyorkhistoryblog.org/2014/09/the-sinking-of-the-s-s-normandie-at-nycs-pier-88/
2. Micheal L. Grace, Cruise Ship History: The French Line's SS NORMANDIE. The greatest liner ever to sail "across the pond"! Will the SS United States and QE 2 face a similar demise? (February 18, 2009)
3. Cristina Vignone, The Rich and Famous Creating a Buzz for Normandie, Fordham (November 10, 2014), https://www.fordham.edu/normandie/people/CV3%20The%20Rich%20and%20Famous%20Creating%20a%20Buzz%20for%20Normandie.html
4. Lorraine B. Diehl, Smoke Over Manhattan: The Fate of the SS Normandie, World War II Magazine (March/April 2010), https://www.historynet.com/the-fate-of-the-ss-normandie.htm
5. Emily S. Reub, The Normandie Breathes Again, New York Times (June 4, 2010), available at https://cityroom.blogs.nytimes.com/2010/06/04/the-normandie-breathes-again/
6. James Barron, Shrine to a Special Ship is Given to a Public Display, New York Times,(February 2, 2010), available at https://cityroom.blogs.nytimes.com/2010/02/02/shrine-to-a-special-ship-is-given-to-a-public-display/
7. https://en.wikipedia.org/wiki/SS_Normandie

Images Source

1. https://www.hrmm.org/history-blog/media-monday-the-ss-normandie-fire-1942

2. httpscommons.wikimedia.orgwikiFilePostal_card_of_the_ocean_liner_Normandie.jpg

3. https://www.reddit.com/r/ArtDeco/comments/7vp69c/ss_normandie_dining_room_1935/

SS Liberté

1. Michael L. Grace, The French Line- SS Liberte'- 1950s, Cruise Line History (Oct 8, 2009), https://www.cruiselinehistory.com/the-french-line-ss-Liberte'-1950s/
2. Nazi Group Organized on S.S. Europa, Jewish Telegraphic Agency Bulletin (Mar 23,1933), https://www.jta.org/1933/03/23/archive/nazi-group-organized-on-s-s-europa
3. Michael L. Grace, The SS Europa and Celebrities who crossed the Pond Aboard the Great German Liner- From Schiaparelli to Riefenstahl, https://www.cruiselinehistory.com/the-ss-europa-and-celebrities-who-crossed-the-pond-aboard-the-great-german-liner-from-schiaparelli-to-riefenstahl/
4. Wikipedia https://en.wikipedia.org/wiki/SS-Europa-(1928)
5. http://www.relevantsearchscotland.co.uk/ships/ships/038europa.html
6. http://www.thegreatoceanliners.com/europa.html

Images Source

1. https://en.wikipedia.org/wiki/SS_Europa_(1928)#/media/File:Bundesarchiv_Bild_102-09251,_Hamburg,_Probefahrt_der_%22Europa%22.jpg
2. https://www.facebook.com/photo?fbid=580954065642976&set=ecnf.100068915156108

SS France

SS France **(1896)**

https://en.wikipedia.org/wiki/SS_France_(1896)

https://www.wikiwand.com/en/SS_France

SS France **(1912)**

https://www.ggarchives.com/OceanTravel/Brochures/CGT-FrLine-1912-SteamshipFrance.html

https://greatships.net/france2

https://store.titanichistoricalsociety.org/product/ss-france-1912/

SS France **(1960)**

1. Martin Cox, *SS France*, *SS Norway*, April 4, 2010, Maritime Matters
2. The Pride of a Nation: Luxury liner that's set to sail once more, The Independent, 26th February, 2011.
3. *SS France* (1960)Wikipedia https://en.wikipedia.org/wiki/SS_France_(1960)
4. The *SS France* and the *SS Liberty*–Elegance at Sea–Now a memory https://www.cruiselinehistory.com/the-ss-france-and-the-ss-Liberte'-elegance-at-sea-now-a-memory/
5. Captains Voyage.com–SS France–Trans Atlantic Services and Cruises http://www.captainsvoyage.com/norwegian-cruise-line/ss-norway/ss-france–trans-atlantic.html
6. Captains Voyage.com, Timeline–The very beginning–why the France was built http://www.captainsvoyage.com/norwegian-cruise-line/ss-norway/timeline.html
7. The End of NCL's SS Norway http://malcolmoliver.files.wordpress.com/2008/07/norway profile.jpg
8. Beyond Ships, *SS Norway* (*SS France*) Profile https://www.beyondships1.com/ss-norway-profile.html

Images Source

1. https://www.pinterest.com/pin/161848180329444003)
2. https://en.wikipedia.org/wiki/SS_France_(1960)

Mona Lisa

1. Lisa Liebmann, Jackie, JFK and the art of diplomacy, Tate (Issue 6: Spring 2006), https://www.tate.org.uk/tate-etc/issue-6-spring-2006/jackie-jfk-and-art-diplomacy
2. Barbara Maranzani, A First Lady Brings a French Icon to American Shores, History.com (Jan 8, 2013), https://www.history.com/news/a-first-lady-brings-a-french-icon-to-american-shores
3. Aleksandr Gelfand, Today in Met History: February 4 (2013), https://www.metmuseum.org/blogs/now-at-the-met/features/2013/today-in-met-history-february-4
4. Margaret Leslie Davis, The Two First Ladies, Vanity Fair (Nov 2008), https://www.vanityfair.com/news/2008/11/monalisa_excerpt200811
5. How the Mona Lisa Came to Camelot, Sunday Times Magazine (Dec 7, 2008)

Images Source

1. https://pinkerton.com/our-insights/blog/mona-lisa-and-the-pinkertons-1962-63
2. https://www.metmuseum.org/articles/today-in-met-history-february-4

   https://en.
3. https://en.wikipedia.org/wiki/Mona_Lisa#/media/File:Mona_Lisa,_by_Leonardo_da_Vinci,_from_C2RMF_retouched.jpg.

Salvadore Dali

1. Olivia Singer, The Surrealist Scent of Salvador Dali, An Other Magazine (Nov 17, 2015), The Surrealist Scent of Salvador Dalí | An Other
2. Daisy Woodward, Salvador Dalí's Ocelot, An Other Magazine (Jan 23, 2015), Salvador Dalí's Ocelot | An Other,
3. Patrick James, Surreal Times on the *SS France*, BBC News (Jun 12 2006), BBC NEWS | Europe | Surreal times on the SS France,
4. Cutterandcutter.com/art/salvadore-dali/mythology-the-judgment-of-paris/

   https://www.cutterandcutter.com/

Images Source

1. https://en.m.wikipedia.org/wiki/File:Salvador_Dali_NYWTS.jpg

Le Clemenceau

1. French Aircraft Carrier Clemenceau
https://en.wikipedia.org/wiki/French_aircraft_carrier_Clemenceau
2. French Apex Court rules, Clemenceau recalled
https://indiatogether.org/shipretn-environment
3. French aircraft carrier Clemenceau (R98)
https://military-history.fandom.com/wiki/French_aircraft_carrier_Clemenceau_(R98)
4. French Navy / Marine Nationale - Aircraft Carrier R 98 FS Clemenceau
https://www.seaforces.org/marint/French-Navy/Aircraft-Carrier/R-98-FS-Clemenceau.htm
5. Marcos A. Orellana : Shipbreaking and Le Clemenceau Row
American Society of International Law https://www.asil.org/insights/volume/10/issue/4/shipbreaking-and-le-clemenceau-row
6. *The Clemenceau* : asbestos could have been removed in France, Address to the Monitoring Committee of the Indian Supreme Court New Delhi, 20th January, 2006, Annie Thébaud-Mony Spokeswoman for Ban Asbestos France and the International Federation for Human Rights (FIDH)
https://www.fidh.org/IMG/pdf/clem20012006a.pdf
7. Chirac orders carrier back to France
https://www.nytimes.com/2006/02/15/world/europe/chirac-orders-carrier-back-to-france.html
8. Contaminated aircraft carrier finds final resting place in Hartlepool Asbestos-ridden Clemenceau was once the pride of the French navy and was used in the first Gulf war
https://www.theguardian.com/environment/2009/feb/06/clemenceau-ghost-ship-teesside

Images Source

1. https://commons.wikimedia.org/wiki/File:FS_Clemenceau_%28R98%29_side_view.jpg

Notes

Part-I: Beginnings

1. **Charles de Gaulle**, (born Nov. 22, 1890, Lille, France – died Nov. 9, 1970), was a French soldier, statesman, and architect of France's Fifth Republic. He joined the army in 1913 and fought with distinction in World War I. When an insurrection in Algeria threatened to bring civil war to France, he returned to power in 1958, as prime minister with powers to reform the Constitution. That same year he was elected president of the new Fifth Republic, which ensured a strong presidency. After the civil unrest of May 1968 by students and workers, he was defeated in a referendum on constitutional amendments and resigned in 1969. *Brittanica.com*

2. **Compagnie Generale Transatlantique** typically known overseas as the French Line, was a French shipping company. Established in 1855 by the brothers Émile and IssacPéreire under the name *Compagnie Générale Maritime*, the company was entrusted by the French government to transport mail to North America. In 1861, the name of the company was changed to *Compagnie Générale Transatlantique. Wikipedia*

3. **Saint Nazaire** is a town in Western France. It has a major harbour on the right bank of the Loire River estuary, near the Atlantic Ocean. It has a long tradition of fishing and ship breaking. *Wikipedia*

4. **Keel** is the bottom-most structural member around which the hull of a ship is built. The keel runs along the centerline of the ship, from the bow to the stern. The keel is often the first part of a ship's hull to be constructed, and laying the keel, or placing the keel in the cradle in which the ship will be built may mark the start time of its construction. *Wikipedia*

5. **Le Havre** was founded on October 8, 1517 as a new port. It is the second largest commercial port in northern France's *Normandie* region, where the river Seine meets the English Channel. *Wikipedia*

6. **Canary Islands** is a set of islands located in the southernmost region of Spain. Being of volcanic origin, they are closer to Africa. Among the islands, especially Tenerife, Gran Canaria, Fuerteventura, and Lanzarote, are a major tourist destination, with over 12 million visitors per year. This is due to their beaches, subtropical climate, and important natural attractions, especially Maspalomas in Gran Canaria and Mount Teide (a World Heritage Site) in Tenerife. Mount Teide is the highest peak in Spain and the third tallest volcano in the world, measured from its base on the ocean floor. *Wikipedia*

7. **RMS (Royal Mail Ship) Titanic** was a British passenger liner, operated by the White Star Line, which sank in the North Atlantic Ocean on 15th April, 1912 after striking an iceberg during her maiden voyage on 10th April, 1912 from Southampton, England, to New York City, United States. Of the estimated 2,224 passengers and crew aboard, more than 1,500 died, making it the deadliest sinking of a single ship up to that time. *Wikipedia*

8. **Great Depression** was a "worldwide economic downturn that began in 1929 and lasted until about 1939.It was the longest and most severe depression ever experienced by the industrialised western world..." *Brittanica.com.*

9. **Hermaphroditus** is the two-sexed child of Aphrodite and Hermes (Venus and Mercury) has long been a symbol of androgyny or effeminacy and was portrayed in Greco-Roman art as a female figure with male genitals. *Wikipedia.*

10. **Albert François Lebrun** (29th August, 1871–6th March, 1950) was a French politician, President of France from 1932 to 1940. *Wikipedia.*

11. **Blue Ribband** is an accolade given to the passenger ship that held the fastest record for transatlantic crossing. *Wikipedia.*

12. **RMS Queen Mary** was a retired British ocean liner that sailed primarily on the North Atlantic Ocean from 1936 to 1967 for the Cunard-White Star Line and was built by John Brown & Company in Clydebank, Scotland. *Queen Mary* sailed on her maiden voyage on 27th May, 1936 and won the Blue Riband that August; she lost the title to SS *Normandie* in 1937 and recaptured it in 1938, holding it until 1952, when it was taken by the new SS *United States*. With the outbreak of World War II, she was converted into a troopship and ferried Allied soldiers during

the conflict. *Queen Mary*, along with RMS *Queen Elizabeth*, was built as part of Cunard's planned two-ship weekly express service between Southampton, Cherbourg and New York. The two ships were a British response to the express superliners built by German, Italian and French companies in the late 1920s and early 1930s. It served as a transatlantic liner, troop transporter and cruise ship until 1967 when it was docked permanently at the Port of Long Beach, California to serve as a hotel and conference centre. *Wikipedia*

13. **Pearl Harbor** is a U.S. naval base near Honolulu, Hawaii, that was the scene of a devastating surprise attack by Japanese forces on December 7, 1941. Just before 8 a.m. on that Sunday morning, hundreds of Japanese fighter planes descended on the base, where they managed to destroy and damage nearly 20 American naval vessels, including eight battleships, and over 300 airplanes. More than 2,400 Americans died in the attack, including civilians, and another 1,000 people were wounded. The day after the assault, President Franklin D. Roosevelt asked Congress to declare war on Japan. *History.com*

14. **Marie-Joseph Paul Yves Roch Gilbert du Motier de La Fayette, Marquis de La Fayette** (6th September, 1757 – 20th May, 1834) known in the United States as **Lafayette** was a French aristocrat, freemason, and military officer who fought in the American Revolutionary War, commanding American troops in several battles, including the siege of Yorktown. After returning to France, he was a key figure in the French Revolution of 1789 and the July Revolution of 1830. He has been considered a national hero in both countries. *Wikipedia*

15. **Reparation Commission-** After World War II both West Germany and East Germany were obliged to pay war reparations to the Allied governments, in accordance with the Potsdam Conference. Other Axis Nations were obliged to pay war reparations according to the Paris Peace Treaties, 1947. Austria was not included in any of these treaties. *Britannica.com*

16. **Catapult** - An aircraft catapult is a device used to allow aircraft to take off in a limited distance, typically from the deck of a vessel. *Wikipedia*

17. **Operation Sealion** was the code name for Nazi Germany's planned invasion of Britain. Had it been successful, it would have completed Adolf Hitler's domination of western Europe. Hitler postponed operation Sea Lion indefinitely on 17 September 1940 and it was never put into action. *Wikipedia*

18. **Orkney Islands** is an archipelago in the Northern Isles of Scotland, situated off the north coast of the island of Great Britain. *Wikipedia*

19. **SS Paris** was a French ocean liner built for the Compagnie Générale Transatlantique by Chantiers de l'Atlantique in Saint-Nazaire, France. *Wikipedia*

Part-II: Meeting Mona Lisa

20. **Mona Lisa-** Leonardo da Vinci's iconic Mona Lisa was painted between 1503 and 1519. It is an oil painting on a poplar wood panel, probably the world's most famous painting. It was owned by French royalty for centuries. Liberated by Revolutionary forces, the painting briefly adorned Napoleon's bedroom and then was installed in the Louvre. Over 80% of Louvre visitors come specifically to see the Mona Lisa. Thought by most scholars to be a portrait of Italian noble woman Lisa del Giocondo, this beautiful, dark-haired woman with an enigmatic gaze has fascinated people for ages. Unlike most 16th-century portraits of nobility, which showed off their social status and wealth with flamboyant clothing, hairstyles and accessories, Mona Lisa is dressed in elegant simplicity, which draws attention to her face. The sitter's mysterious smile and her unproven identity have made the painting a source of ongoing investigation and fascination. *artandobject.com and Wikipedia.*

21. **Jacqueline Lee Bouvier** popularly known as "Jackie" was born on July 28, 1929, in Southampton, New York to Wall Street stockbroker John Vernou "Black Jack" Bouvier III and socialite Janet Norton Lee. Her mother was of Irish descent, and her father had French, Scottish, and English ancestry. After graduating with a Bachelor of Arts in French literature from George Washington University in 1951, Jacqueline started working for the Washington Times-Herald as an inquiring photographer. The following year, she met then-Congressman John Kennedy at a dinner party in Washington. He was elected to the Senate that same year, and the couple married on September 12, 1953, in Newport, Rhode Island. They had four children, two of whom died in infancy. She served as the first lady of the United States from 1961 to 1963, as the wife of President John F. Kennedy, the 35th President of the United States.

    After the assassination of her husband in 1963, Kennedy and her children largely withdrew from public view. In 1968, she married the Greek shipping magnate Aristotle Onassis, who was one of the wealthiest men in the world. Her marriage to Aristotle Onassis caused her popularity to decline sharply among the American public who viewed it as a betrayal of the assassinated president. Onassis died in 1975. Thereafter, Jacqueline took conscious control of her public image and, by the time of her death, succeeded in rehabilitating it. By moving back to New York City after Onassis's death, she opted to work as an editor for Viking Press and Doubleday. Her focus was on her children and grandchildren and her contribution to charitable causes. All these activities restored her reputation. She also re-established her relationship with the Kennedy family and supported the John F. Kennedy Library and Museum. She died on May 19, 1994, in New York City. *Wikipedia.*

22. **André Malraux** in full André-Georges Malraux, (born on Nov. 3, 1901, Paris, France - died Nov. 23, 1976, Paris), French novelist, art historian, and statesman who became an active supporter of Gen. Charles de Gaulle and, after de Gaulle was elected president in 1958, served for 10 years as France's minister of cultural affairs. His major works include the novel *La Condition Humaine* (1933; *Man's Fate*); *Les Voix du silence* (1951; *The Voices of Silence*), a history and philosophy of world art; and *Le Muséeimaginaire de la sculpture mondiale* (1952–54; *Museum Without Walls*). *Brittanica.com*

23. **The Louvre** is a national art museum in Paris, France. A central landmark of the city, it is located on the right bank of the Seine and is home to some of the most canonical works of Western art, including the Mona Lisa and the Venus de Milo. The museum is housed in the Louvre Palace, originally built in the late 12th to 13th century under Philip II. Remnants of the Medieval Louvre fortress are visible in the basement of the museum. Due to urban expansion, the fortress eventually lost its defensive function, and in 1546 Francis I converted it into the primary residence of the French Kings.

    The museum opened on 10th August, 1793, with an exhibition of 537 paintings, the majority of the works being royal and confiscated church property. Because of structural problems with the building, the museum was closed in 1796 until 1801. The collection was increased under Napoleon and the museum was renamed Musée Napoléon, but after Napoleon's abdication, many works seized by his armies were returned to their original owners. The collection was further increased during the reigns of Louis XVIII and Charles X, and during the Second French

Empire, the museum gained 20,000 pieces. Holdings have grown steadily through donations and bequests since the Third Republic. The collection is divided among eight curatorial departments: Egyptian Antiquities; Near Eastern Antiquities; Greek, Etruscan, and Roman Antiquities; Islamic Art; Sculpture; Decorative Arts; Paintings; Prints and Drawing. *Wikipedia*

24. **Vincenzo Peruggia** (8th October, 1881– 8th October, 1925) was an Italian museum worker, artist and thief, most famous for stealing the Mona Lisa from the Louvre Museum in Paris on 21st August, 1911. In 1911, Peruggia perpetrated what has been described as the greatest art theft of the 20th century. It was a police theory that the former Louvre worker hid inside the museum on Sunday, 20th August, knowing the museum would be closed the following day. But, according to Peruggia's interrogation in Florence after his arrest, he entered the museum on Monday, 21st August, around 7 am, through the door from which the other Louvre workers were entering. He said he wore one of the white smocks that the museum employees customarily wore and was indistinguishable from the other workers. When the Salon Carré, where the Mona Lisa hung, was empty, he lifted the painting off the four iron pegs that secured it to the wall and took it to a nearby service staircase. There, he removed the protective case and frame. Some people report that he concealed the painting (which Leonardo painted on wood) under his smock. But Peruggia was only 160 centimetres (63 in) tall, and the Mona Lisa measured approx. 53 cm × 77 cm (21 in × 30 in), so it would not fit under a smock worn by someone his size. Instead, he said he took off his smock and wrapped it around the painting, tucked it under his arm, and left the Louvre through the same door he had entered. Peruggia hid the painting in his apartment in Paris.

After keeping the painting hidden in a trunk in his apartment for two years, Peruggia returned to Italy with it. He kept it in his apartment in Florence, Italy for some time. However, Peruggia eventually grew impatient and was finally caught when he contacted Mario Fratelli, the owner of an art gallery in Florence. Fratelli's story conflicts with Peruggia's, but it was clear that Peruggia expected a reward for returning the painting to what he regarded as its "homeland". Fratelli called in Giovanni Poggi, Director of the Uffizi Gallery, who authenticated the painting. Poggi and Fratelli, after taking the painting for "safekeeping", informed the police, who arrested Peruggia at his hotel. After its recovery, the painting was exhibited all over Italy with banner headlines rejoicing its return. The Mona Lisa was then returned to the Louvre in 1913. While the painting was famous before the theft, the notoriety it received from the newspaper headlines and the large scale police investigation helped the artwork become one of the best known in the world, gaining considerable public interest.

There are currently two predominant theories regarding the theft of the Mona Lisa. Peruggia said he did it for a patriotic reason: he wanted to bring the painting back for display in Italy "after it was stolen by Napoleon" (when Peruggia worked at the Louvre, he learned of how Napoleon plundered many Italian works of art during the Napoleonic Wars). Although perhaps sincere in his motive, Vincenzo may not have known that Leonardo da Vinci took this painting as a gift for Francis I when he moved to France to become a painter in his court during the 16th century, 250 years before Napoleon's birth.

Experts have questioned the 'patriotism' motive on the grounds that—if 'patriotism' was the true motive—Peruggia would have donated the painting to an Italian museum, rather than have attempted to profit from its sale. The question of money is also confirmed by letters that Peruggia sent to his father after the theft. On 22nd December, 1911, four months after the theft, he wrote that Paris was where "I will make my fortune and that his (fortune) will arrive in one shot." The following year (1912), he wrote: "I am making a vow for you to live long and enjoy the prize that your son is about to realize for you and all our family."

Put on trial, the court agreed, to some extent, that Peruggia committed his crime for patriotic reasons and gave him a lenient sentence. He was sent to jail for one year and 15 days but was hailed as a great patriot in Italy and served only seven months in jail.

Another theory emerged later. The theft may have been encouraged or masterminded by Eduardo de Valfierno, a con man who had commissioned the French art forger Yves Chaudron to make copies of the painting so he could sell them as the missing original. The copies would have gone up in value if the original were stolen. This theory is based entirely on a 1932 article by former Hearst journalist Karl Decker in The Saturday Evening Post. Decker claimed to have known Valfierno and heard the story from him in 1913, promising not to print it until he learned of Valfierno's death. There is no external confirmation for this theory.

Peruggia was released from jail after a short time and served in the Italian army during World War I. During the war, he was captured by Austria-Hungary and held as a POW for two years until the war ended and he was released. He later married, had one daughter, Celestina, returned to France and continued to work as a painter decorator using his birth name Pietro Peruggia. He died on 8th October 1925 (his 44th birthday) in the Paris suburb of Saint-Maur-des-Fossés, France. He was buried in the Condé Cemetery of Saint-Maur-des-Fossés. Sometime in the 1950s, Peruggia's remains were exhumed and relocated into the cemetery. *Wikipedia*

25. **Surrealism** movement in visual art and literature, flourished in Europe between World Wars I and II. Surrealism grew principally out of the earlier Dada movement, which before World War I produced works of anti-art that deliberately defied reason; but Surrealism's emphasis was not on negation but on positive expression. The movement represented a reaction against what its members saw as the destruction wrought by "rationalism" that had guided European culture and politics in the past and that had culminated in the horrors of World War I. According to the major spokesman of the movement, the poet and critic André Breton, who published The Surrealist Manifesto in 1924, Surrealism was a means of reuniting conscious and unconscious realms of experience so completely that the world of dream and fantasy would be joined to the everyday rational world in "an absolute reality, a surreality." Drawing heavily on theories adapted from Sigmund Freud, Breton saw the unconscious as the wellspring of the imagination. He defined genius in terms of accessibility to this normally untapped realm, which, he believed, could be attained by poets and painters alike. *Britannica.com*

26. **Salvador Dali** was born on 11th May, 1904 in Spain. He came closer to surrealism in 1920 and later joined the surrealist group in 1929. He died on 23rd January, 1989. There are two major museums devoted to his work: The Dalí Theatre-Museum in Figueres, Spain and the Salvador Dalí Museum in Florida. *Wikipedia*

    "Salvador Dalí is among the most versatile and prolific artists of the 20th century and the most famous Surrealist. Though chiefly remembered for his painterly output, in the course of his long career he successfully turned to sculpture, printmaking, fashion, advertising, writing, and, perhaps most famously, filmmaking in his collaborations with Luis Buñuel and Alfred Hitchcock. Dalí was renowned for his flamboyant personality and role of mischievous provocateur as much as for his undeniable technical virtuosity. In his early use of organic morphology, his work bears the stamp of fellow Spaniards Pablo Picasso and Joan Miró. His paintings also evince a fascination for Classical and Renaissance art, clearly visible through his hyper-realistic style and religious symbolism of his later work."

One of his famous quotes: " The fact that I myself, at the moment of painting, do not understand my own pictures, does not mean that these pictures have no meaning; on the contrary, their meaning is so profound, complex, and involuntary that it escapes the most simple analysis of logical intuition." *Theartstory.org*

27. **The ocelot** *(Leopardus pardalis)*, also known as the dwarf leopard or McKenney's wildcat, is a species of wild cat found predominantly in South and Central America. It is similar in appearance to a domestic cat, although its fur resembles that of a clouded leopard or jaguar. From 1972 to 1997, this sleek, smooth coating led to the ocelot's status as an endangered species after thousands were killed and their fur sold at great expense. Ocelot coat patterns can vary greatly, being anything from cream to grey to reddish-brown in colour and marked with black rosettes; while their ears are rounded, their tails long and their front paws large. The species is mainly nocturnal, with incredibly good vision, and is very territorial, fighting fiercely (sometimes to the death) in territorial disputes. Dalí acquired his ocelot Babou in the 1960s (allegedly from the Colombian Head of State), and for a time it was seen to accompany him, on a leash and stone studded collar, almost everywhere he went. *Anothermag.com*

28. **Michel Sardou** was born on 26th January, 1947, in Paris. His father, Fernand Sardou, was a singer and an actor while his mother, Jackie Sardou was an actress. His paternal grandfather, Valentin Sardou, was a comedian in Marseille, while his grandmother was a singer. Sardou left school at the age 16. He is known not only for his love songs ("La maladie d'amour", "Je vaist'aimer"), but also for songs dealing with various social and political issues, such as the rights of women in Islamic countries ("Musulmanes"), clerical celibacy ("Le curé"), colonialism

("Le temps des colonies", "Ilsont le pétrolemaisc'est tout") or the death penalty ("Je suis pour"). *Wikipedia*

His poem on the *Blue Lady* became very popular:

The "France"

When I think of the old English lady
that was called the *Queen Mary*,
as she lays beached so far away from her cliffs
on a wharf in California

When I think of the old English lady,
I envy the submerged wrecks,
liners that were chasing a dream
and never saw their country again.

Don't ever call me *France* again,
France has just left me in the lurch
Don't ever call me *France* again,
this is my last will.

I was a gigantic ship,
able to cruise for a thousand years.
I was a giant, I was nearly,
nearly as strong as the ocean.

I was a gigantic ship,
I carried thousands of lovers.
I was France. What remains of it?
A perch for seagulls

Don't ever call me *France* again

France has just left me in the lurch
Don't ever call me *France* again,
this is my last will.

When I think of the old English lady
that was called the *Queen Mary*,
as she lays beached so far away from her cliffs

on a wharf in California.
Let the mightiest warship
be brave enough to sink me,
while i'll show my ass to Saint-Nazaire,
in the land of Britanny where I was born.
Don't ever call me *France* again,
France has just left me in the lurch
Don't ever call me *France* again,
this is my last will.

Part-III: Turn of Events

29. **RMS Queen Elizabeth** was an ocean liner operated by Cunard Line. With Queen Mary she provided weekly luxury liner service between Southampton in the United Kingdom and New York City in the United States, via Cherbourg in France. While being constructed in the mid-1930s by John Brown and Company at Clydebank, Scotland, the build was known as *Hull 552*. She was launched on 27th September, 1938, and named in honour of Queen Elizabeth, later known as the Queen Mother. With a design that improved upon that of *Queen Mary*, *Queen Elizabeth* was slightly larger being 12 feet longer than her sister ship, she was the largest passenger liner ever built at that time and for 56 years thereafter. She also has the distinction of being the largest-ever riveted ship by gross tonnage. She first entered service in February 1940 as a troopship in the Second World War, and it was not until October 1946 that she served in her intended role as an ocean liner. *Wikipedia*
30. **The Basel Convention** on the "Control of Transboundary Movements of Hazardous Wastes and their Disposal" was adopted on 22nd March,1989 by the Conference of Plenipotentiaries in Basel, Switzerland, in response to a public outcry following the discovery, in the 1980s, in Africa and other parts of the developing world of deposits of toxic wastes imported from abroad. The provisions of the Convention centre around the following principal aims:
    - the reduction of hazardous waste generation and the promotion of environmentally sound management of hazardous wastes, wherever the place of disposal;
    - the restriction of transboundary movements of hazardous wastes

except where it is perceived to be in accordance with the principles of environmentally sound management; and

- a regulatory system applying to cases where transboundary movements are permissible.
- The Convention provides a framework to check transboundary movement of hazardous waste in the international boundaries, in particular by the OECD countries to Non-OECD countries.

Based on the concept of prior informed consent, it requires that before an export may take place, the authorities of the State of export notify the authorities of the prospective States of import and transit, providing them with detailed information on the intended movement. The movement may only proceed if and when all States concerned have given their written consent (Articles 6 and 7). Basel Convention was signed and ratified by the European Union and several other countries. India signed the Convention on 5.5.1992 and ratified it on 24.6.1992. The Convention entered into force in 1992. Parties to the Basel Convention have been concerned about the issue of ship dismantling for the past decade as end-of-life ships comprise an array of hazardous materials such as asbestos, PCB and waste oils which can have serious implications for the environment and human health if not managed properly. As ships destined for dismantling will rarely fly the flag of the State in which they are to be recycled, this activity can represent a transboundary movement of hazardous waste. At the seventh meeting of the Conference of the Parties in 2004, while Basel Parties recognized that ship may become waste as defined in Article 2 of the Basel Convention, they also invited the International Maritime Organization (IMO) to continue work aimed at the establishment of mandatory requirements to ensure the environmentally sound management of ship dismantling (decision VII/26 on environmentally sound management of ship dismantling). The Hong Kong International Convention for the Safe and Environmentally Sound Recycling of Ships was adopted at a diplomatic conference in Hong Kong, China, in May 2009. Following this, in May 2010, the seventh session of the Open-ended Working Group welcomed the adoption of the Hong Kong Convention and developed criteria necessary to carry out a preliminary assessment of equivalency (decision OEWG-VII/12 on Environmentally sound dismantling of ships). When Parties met for the tenth meeting of the Conference of the Parties in Cartagena,

Colombia, consensus on whether there is an equivalent level of control and enforcement between the Basel and Hong Kong conventions could not be reached. Nevertheless, the Conference of the Parties encouraged parties to ratify the Hong Kong Convention to enable its early entry into force. COP 10 also acknowledged that the Basel Convention should continue to assist countries to apply the Basel Convention as it relates to ships (decision BC-10/17 on Environmentally sound dismantling of ships).

On the matter of international cooperation and technical assistance activities concerning ship recycling, decision BC-10/17 requested the Secretariat, subject to the availability of funding, to develop further the programmes for sustainable ship recycling in conjunction with other bodies, in particular the IMO and the ILO. *Basel Convention*

31. Inter-Ministerial Committee of Bangladesh in its meeting dated 15.2.2006 refused the entry of *S.S. Norway* or under any other name, on the ground that under the Basel Convention, the Signatory Country has a right to refuse any material or carrier which can cause harm to the environment.[(A-2)] Later, the Supreme Court of Bangladesh gave a judgment dated 27.4.2009 holding that decommissioned sea-going vessels, including end-of-life single-hull oil tankers which have been destined for disposal recycling, are being sent from European and other countries to be dismantled in Bangladesh without first being decontaminated of hazardous material as is required by the Basel Convention. Thereby upholding prior decontimination before export of a ship for dismantling.

32. The Supreme Court of India appointed a High Powered Committee (HPC) with Professor MGK Menon, an eminent scientist, as its Chairperson by order dated 13.10.1997. The HPC was assigned 14 terms of reference on which it was required to give its report and recommendations. With regard to ship breaking, the issue was: "14. Decontamination of ships before they are exported to India for breaking."

33. The HPC, during its visit, found that no landfill site was available at Alang for disposal of the waste in an environmentally sound manner and that the toxic waste was thrown and burnt indiscriminately at the beach. Photographs of these unhealthy practices were enclosed with the Report. The Report with regard to the ship breaking activities recommended that the ships destined for ship breaking on India's coasts must provide a

complete inventory of the hazardous wastes; ships destined for breaking ought to be decontaminated and that as far as the handling of hazardous wastes including asbestos is concerned, it should follow uniform international standards. It further recommended that merely because workers in Alang are from poorer strata of society, they cannot be denied the same rights as workers in other countries enjoy. The workers should be fully protected and their health be monitored. HPC was shocked that approx. 40 deaths every year take place due to accidents and other causes associated with ship-breaking activities. Central Pollution Control Board had taken an independent stand on 29.2.2000 in its affidavit before the Supreme Court that it is required to be ensured that "the ships are properly decontaminated before export to India."

34. "Alang Sosiya Yard" is located on the Coast of Gulf of Cambay, on the west coast of India, 50 km from Bhavnagar (Gujarat, India). It is the world's biggest ship-breaking yard. One Capt. N. Sundaresan (1933–2012) is said to be the founder of Alang Ship Recycling Yard. He was a Master mariner and had a sense of identifying what would be the best site for ship breaking and thus chose the present site at Alang for ship recycling. The first vessel – MV Kota Tenjong was beached at Alang on 13th February, 1983. Since then, the place witnessed spectacular growth. The place was found proper for ship-breaking owing to the high tidal range, gentle seaward gradient and firm holding ground. The place is recognized at present as a leading ship-breaking yard in the world. Village-Alang has a big market starting from Tapaz village, where various articles that come out during ship-dismantling like furniture, electrical appliances, boats, washing machines etc. are sold. The market spreads over an area of nearly 10 km, starting from Tapaz village. *Alanginfo.com*

35. The Research Foundation for Science Technology and Ecology (RFSTE) which later became Research Foundation for Science Technology and, Natural Resource Policy, an NGO, filed a writ petition under Article 32 of the Constitution for enforcement of the fundamental right to clean environment under Article 21 before the Supreme Court of India to prevent dumping of hazardous wastes by the developed countries in various forms and for implementation of the Basel Convention as a part of municipal law, which was signed by India on 15.03.1990 and ratified on 24.06.1992. The Convention, inter alia, provided "prior informed

consent" regarding the transboundary movement of hazardous wastes and their disposal in an environmentally sound manner.

Order dated 14.10.2003 (RFSTE Vs UOI) by the Supreme Court of India giving several directions. The Court declared that the Basel Convention effectuates the Fundamental Right guaranteed under Article 21 of the Constitution and therefore, to be read as a part of it. The Court also accepted that Principles 4,10 and 19 of the Rio Declaration also form part of Article 21. About ship breaking, the order clearly directed that before a ship arrives at the port, it should have proper consent from the authority concerned or the state maritime board, stating that it does not contain any hazardous wastes or radioactive substances. A ship should be properly decontaminated by the ship owner prior to breaking, which should be ensured by the State Pollution Control Boards. No breaking permission should be granted unless there is a complete inventory of hazardous wastes on board the ship. Further, at the international level India should participate in the implementation of the Basel Convention with a clear mandate for the decontamination of ships of their hazardous substances such as asbestos, waste oil, gas and PCBs, prior to export to India for breaking. *RFSTE Vs UOI (2005) 10 SCC 510* [Excerpts **A- 11**]

Part IV: The Story of *SS Clemenceau*

36. The Supreme Court passed an order on 16.1.2006 that till the next date of hearing, the *Clemenceau* shall not be permitted to enter the Exclusive Economic Zone. The Ministry of Environment and Forests had taken a clear stand as mentioned in its affidavit filed before the Supreme Court that "ships prior to dismantling should be decontaminated to the extent possible."

37. While the *Clemenceau* was on its way, the Supreme Court had allowed by its order dated 13.2.2006, the Customs Authority to examine whether hazardous substances are present and whether it would be desirable to permit the ship to come to the Exclusive Economic Zone. There were many articles written about the *Clemenceau* and public demonstrations that the *Clemenceau* should not be allowed in India for breaking. The Supreme Court passed a very strange order on 13.2.2006 itself that If any person will write or demonstrate, "he shall be prima facie held to have committed contempt of this court and appropriate action shall be taken against him."

38. Order dated 17.2.2006 of the Supreme Court recording that the French Government had recalled the *Clemenceau*. However, to examine whether there are sufficient facilities for ship breaking at Alang, it constituted a Technical Expert Committee (TEC) to make comprehensive recommendations on ship breaking.

[The Clemenceau was finally bought by a company "Able UK" and taken to the shipbreaking yard, Graythorp, within Hartlepool Port in north-eastern England in early February 2009. This time nobody raised any protest, as the destruction was being carried out in Europe itself. The dismantling process started on 18th November 2009 and was over by the end of 2010.]

PART V: Final Days

39. Application (I.A. No. 29/2006 in W.P. NO. 657/1995) was filed by the Environmental Activist-Gopal Krishna on 11.5.2006 praying that *Blue Lady,* which was heading towards Indian Territorial Waters, be not allowed entry in the Indian Territorial Waters as its entry will be against the directions given by the Supreme Court on 13.10.2003 and Basel Convention.

40. On 12.5.2006, the Supreme Court directed that the grievance in I.A. No. 29/2006 will be examined by the Technical Expert Committee (TEC) already constituted by the Supreme Court. On the same date, the Ministry of Environment and Forest, directed that the ship-Blue Lady should not be allowed to enter the Indian Sovereign jurisdiction till the TEC gives its opinion.

41. Letters dated 15.5.2006 and 17.5.2006 by M/s Haryana Ship Demolition Pvt. Ltd. (who stated to have purchased the ship *Blue Lady* from M/s Bridgend Shipping Ltd.) addressed to the TEC to anchor and beach the ship at Alang coast. In these letters, M/s Haryana Ship said that they were bonafide purchasers. It was admitted that the ship contains 1240 MT of ACM, 85% of which is in the partition walls and ceilings of rooms. It was claimed that the ship was a dead vessel towed by two tugs and that the crew had limited food items besides the unsafe weather conditions.

42. Letter dated 19.5.2006 of the Government of Malaysia stating that SS Norway had left Malaysian waters on 5.5.2006 at 3 pm to Dubai. **(A-3)**

43. The Interim Report was given by the Technical Expert Committee (TEC) in its third meeting dated 20.05.2006 in which the Committee recommended 'anchorage' of the ship. It also recommended beaching by stating that "In the event that M/s GEPIL's report is validated and the vessel is not found to contain any other hazardous materials of a kind or quality which cannot be safely removed, handles and disposed of at Alang, beaching permission may be given."

44. Application (I.A. NO. 30/2006) by the TEC dated 30.05.2006 for considering its Interim Report dated 20.05.2006 and for passing appropriate order regarding anchoring of the ship – *Blue Lady*.

45. Reply dated 03.06.2006 by Gopal Krishna opposing the entry and anchoring of the ship *Blue Lady* in India stating that its entry will violate the Order dated 14.10.2003 of the Supreme Court; that *Blue Lady* contains asbestos more than 2.5 times the amount of asbestos contained in Le Clemenceau. It was also said that Malaysia–the country of export- was obligated to recall *Blue Lady* and that it would be considered 'illegal traffic' under the Basel Convention, as it left Malaysian waters under the guise that it is going for repairs to Dubai.

46. By Order dated 5.6.2006, the Supreme Court accepted the Interim Report of TEC thereby allowing M/s Haryana Ship Demolition Pvt. Ltd. to anchor *Blue Lady* "off-Alang" on humanitarian grounds. However, the order noted that it will not confer any equity in favour of M/s Haryana Ship.

47. On 10.6.2006, the Ministry of Environment granted permission to the *Blue Lady* to anchor "off Alang".

48. On 13.6.2006 instead of anchoring the ship in the Indian Territorial waters, the ship left for Dubai, UAE. There is nothing on record to show whether the *Blue Lady*, which was claimed as a dead ship was towed or sailed by itself. Why anyone will carry the dead ship to Dubai that too contrary to what M/s Haryana Ship claimed in its letters dated 15.5.2006 and 17.5.2006.

49. Report in Khaleej Times dated 30.6.2006 as to how *Blue Lady* after the Supreme Court order dated 5.6.2006, instead of anchoring the ship in the Indian Territorial waters, left for Dubai, UAE and returned and anchored 35 nautical miles away from Alang at Pipavav Port, Gujarat, India **(A-5)**.

On 30.6.2006, *Blue Lady* after the mysterious trip to Dubai returned and anchored 35 nautical miles away from Alang at Pipavav Port, Gujarat, India.

50. Letter dated 8.7.2006 by Gulf Desert-Bleu Ribband to Mr. Ronald – Mike Neumeyer, Senator of Building, Environment and Transportation that they will completely renovate and refurbish *SS Norway* (now *Blue Lady*) as a multi-faceted facility berthed in the UAE indefinitely. It will contain a hotel, shops, restaurants, museum, cultural centre, training academy, etc. This proposal was submitted in view of the international opposition including the pending legal proceedings before the Indian court. This would comply with, as per the letter, the international treaties as well as protect the workers from the hazardous substances and will be a win-win situation–the vessel will find a new and long-lasting life in Dubai.

51. Write-up in Tehelka News dated 23.9.2006 that there were unchecked movements of vessels like the *Blue Lady* and the *Clemenceau* which allowed them to carry contraband, bombs, etc. as per naval intelligence report of late 2004. The report clearly mentioned that some ships that arrive at Alang for dismantling disappear from anchorage after a short while to unknown destinations. The report apprehended that there was a likelihood of ships being involved in nefarious activities. The report went on to allege the involvement of Pakistani nationals – the Dawood gang **(A-7 and A-8).**

52. In a letter dated 31.7.2006, M/s Priya Blue Industries Pvt. Ltd. claimed that they are the new buyer.

53. One M. Subba Rao, an official of Ministry of Environment wrote a letter dated 1.8.2006 asking the Gujarat Maritime Board to proceed further to grant beaching permission to the ship *Blue Lady*.

54. On 15.8.2006, the Gujarat Maritime allowed *Blue Lady* to beach approx. 4000 feet away from the shore. This was done illegally, without permission from the court and in violation of the order dated 14.10.2003 of the Supreme Court.

55. Application (I.A. No.34/2006) by M/s Priya Blue Industries Pvt. Ltd. dated 09.11.2006 requesting the Supreme Court that permission be granted for lightening and dismantling of *Blue Lady* consistent with its earlier order dated 5.6.2006 accepting the interim recommendations.

56. Application (I.A. No.32/2006) filed by Gopal Krishna for directions on 7.8.2006 praying that *Blue Lady* be not permitted to be beached/ broken until the final report of the TEC is submitted and duly considered by the Supreme Court. It was pointed out that due to the presence of toxic material Bangladesh had refused its entry by relying on the Basel Convention. He stated that toxic material is embedded in the structure of *Blue Lady*. He requested that *Blue Lady* be directed to leave the Indian waters at the earliest and in case it was considered for demolition, it should be decontaminated in the country which was equipped to deal with such waste in an environmentally sound manner as per the Basel Convention and thereafter, only it should be allowed to enter into the Indian Territorial Waters. On 15.5.2006, the Supreme Court allowed the ship breaking unit to remove oil from the ship " without claiming any equity"!

57. Letter dated 14.8.2006 by Prof. M.G.K. Menon, who was Chairperson of the High Powered Committee that gave a comprehensive report on ship-breaking, to the then Chief Justice of the Supreme Court against beaching. Professor Menon had said that *Blue Lady* belonged to Star Cruises and it was their responsibility and that of the Government of Malaysia to ensure that the ship was either reconditioned as a maritime liner or to ensure its disposal in an environmentally sound manner as done by the French Government in the case of Clemanceau. He cited the Supreme Court order dated 14th October 2003 and said that any effort to dilute the said order to remove the concept of prior decontamination would be a measure going against the interest of the workers in the ship breaking yards as also a violation of the Basel Convention, both by Malaysia and India who were signatories to the Convention. He made it clear that the only option even if beaching was done was to return the *Blue Lady* to Malaysia **(A-6)**.

58. Order dated 4.12.2006 by the Supreme Court recording the objection of Counsel Mr Sanjay Parikh that the beaching of *Blue Lady* was impermissible. However, the Supreme Court allowed the Pollution Control Board to see whether it would be possible to send back the vessel while examining the dismantling plan.

59. By order dated 12.3.2007, the Supreme Court allowed TEC to examine whether conditions stipulated have been complied with. Thereafter, it was said that "The other aspects relating to the reversibility or

impermissibility of the beaching, manner of dealing with asbestos and other hazardous material shall be considered after the report of the TEC."

60. The TEC submitted its report dated 10.5.2007 recommending grant of permission for dismantling the ship *Blue Lady* at Alang as per the recycling plan submitted by M/s Priya Blue Industries Pvt. Ltd.

61. Letter dated 19.7.2007 by Tom Haugen, involved as a Project Manager in *S.S. Norway* pointing out the presence of Radioactive material in the ship. In his letter dated 9.07.2007 addressed to the TEC he said that he had upgraded the fire detection system of *Blue Lady* in 1990 and that there was a new fire detection system which had approximately 5500 detection points, having 1100 radioactive element Americium 241. He warned that removing Americiun 241 had to be done by skilled persons and all detectors had to be destroyed safely **(A-9).**

    On 26.7.2007, Gopal Krishna- Petitioner, drew the attention of the Supreme Court through an additional affidavit that *Blue Lady* has approximately 5500 fire detection points on board which contain 1100 Radioactive elements- Americium-241, which is a potential health hazard and carcinogenic properties. He also stated that in the dismantling plan submitted by the ship owner, there is no mention of radioactive substances and its safe removal.

62. Inspection Report dated 15/16.8.2007 said that they could find only 12 smoke detectors containing Americiun 241 which were handed over to the ship-breaker Priya Blue for disposal under the supervision of AERB. The team concluded that the ship "now does not contain any radioactive material on board." Thus, 1088 smoke detectors having potentially radioactive substance were left on the ship **(A-10).**

63. Order dated 6.9.2007 by the Supreme Court accepting the final recommendations of the TEC on ship-breaking at Alang and directing Government of India to formulate a comprehensive Code and to amend the statutes to bring them in conformity with the recommendations.

64. Order dated 11.9.2007 by the Supreme Court whereby it accepted the TEC Report dated 10.5.2007 recommending grant of permission for dismantling the ship *Blue Lady* at Alang as per the recycling plan submitted by M/s Priya Blue Industries Pvt. Ltd. and that the process of beaching was irreversible and granted permission to M/s Priya Blue Industries Pvt. Ltd. to dismantle *Blue Lady*. The order said that " 85%

of the asbestos is in the panels and insulation, that quantity is reusable." Except stating that quantity of PCB has been determined by the Gujarat Enviro-protection and Infrastructure Ltd, nothing was said about its disposal in an environmentally sound manner **(A-12).**

- Note dated 11.9.2007 submitted by Mr Sanjay Parikh, Counsel for Mr Gopal Krishna that "It is not safe and against all international norms that any ship without decontamination and prior informed consent is allowed to enter in the territory of our country.....The *Blue Lady* is an example of such an illegality, which should not be allowed to get into the system. Our country should not depart from the procedure, which is followed by all other countries who are members of the Basel Convention."
- The same day, i.e., 11.9.2007, Barry I. Castleman, Sc.D., a known authority on hazardous impacts of asbestos, gave an opinion criticising the Supreme Court for allowing recycling of the hazardous asbestos and called for its reconsideration.

65. December 2007, the tip of *Blue Lady* was cut.

- The Petitioner- Mr Gopal Krishna, moved an application (I.A. 42 of 2007) seeking directions on decontamination and for safe disposal of the radio-active substances, PCB, Asbestos. The Application also asked for any scientific material to show that the beaching was irreversible. There appears to be no order on this application.
- The Committee on Petitions in its 29th Report presented to the Lok Sabha on 22.08.2007 deprecated the stand taken by the MoEF and said: "the Committee strongly deprecates the repeated stand taken by the Ministry that since no hazardous wastes has been allowed on board as cargo there is no violation of the Supreme Court directions. The Committee need not emphasize that the hazardous wastes, whether as cargo or in-built material are equally detrimental to the environment and human health."

Subsequent developments

1. Judgment dated 5/17.3.2009 by the Supreme Court of Bangladesh in BELA Vs Bangladesh, inter alia, directing that vessels containing hazardous materials are not imported without decontamination outside Bangladesh and prior environment clearance is obtained showing that adequate steps

and precautionary measures have been taken. This judgment by the Supreme Court of Bangladesh relied upon the order dated 14.10.2003 passed by the Indian Supreme Court in RFSTE Vs UOI.

2. Considering the fact that the order dated 11.9.2007 had diluted the earlier order dated 14.1.2003 of the Supreme Court, in the written submissions dated 27.1.2012 filed by the Counsel-Mr Sanjay Parikh, it was prayed that the ships should be decontaminated before its export; that declaration about decontamination be sent to the country of import and only after prior informed consent, the ship be allowed; disposal of waste be done in an environmentally sound manner and that verification of the hazardous material on-board of a ship while it has already anchored in the Indian Territorial Waters, is a totally wrong procedure. These submisions were considered in the final judgment dated 06.07.2012.

3. Final judgment in W.P.(C) No. 657/1995 - RFSTE Vs UOI, dated 06.07.2012, wherein the Central Government was directed to ban import of all hazardous/toxic wastes which had been identified and declared to be so under the Basel Convention and its different protocols. The Central Government was also directed to bring the Hazardous Wastes (Management and Handling) Rules, 1989 in line with the Basel Convention and Art. 21, 47, 48A of the Constitution. The judgment also said that "we expect and reiterate that the directions contained in the Basel Convention have to be strictly followed by all the concerned players before a vessel is allowed to enter Indian territorial waters and beached at any of the beaching facilities in any part of the Indian coastline. In case of breach of the conditions, the authorities shall impose the penalties contemplated under the municipal laws of India" **(A-13).**

4. The Hong Kong International Convention for the Safe and Environmentally Sound Recycling of Ships was adopted on 15th May, 2009. It aims at ensuring that ships, when being recycled after reaching the end of their operational lives, do not pose any unnecessary risk to human health and safety or to the environment. The Convention was developed with inputs from the International Labour Organization and the Parties to the Basel Convention on the Control of Transboundary Movements of Hazardous Wastes and their Disposal. Ships to be sent for recycling will be required to carry an inventory of hazardous materials, which will be specific to each ship. Ships will be required to have an initial survey to verify the inventory of hazardous materials, renewal surveys during the life of

the ship, and a final survey prior to recycling. Ship recycling yards will be required to provide a Ship Recycling Plan, to specify the manner in which each individual ship will be recycled, depending on its particulars and its inventory. Parties will be required to take effective measures to ensure that ship recycling facilities under their jurisdiction comply with the Convention.

5. The orders by the Supreme Court on ship recycling led to the framing of a Ship Breaking Code, which was revised in 2013. Later, India being a member of the IMO and having participated in its deliberations, it was decided to adopt the said convention and enact a law based thereon. As a result, the Recycling of Ships Act, 2019 was enacted on 13th December, 2019 by India. *imo.org*

List of Annexures

A-1. Bill of Sale dated 16/19.01.2006 by the Commonwealth of the Bahamas.

A-2. Order by the Government of Bangladesh prohibiting the entry of the *Blue Lady* in its territorial waters, dated 05.02.2006.

A-3. Letter dated 19.05.2006 by the Malaysia Maritime Department

A-4. TOI dated 22.2.2006, "*Blue Lady* is now India's Problem".

A-5. "Did mystery ship owners lie over fate of *SS Norway*" in *Khaleej Times* dated 30.06.2006.

A-6. Letter by MGK Menon dated 14.08.2006 to the then Chief Justice of India, Y.K. Sabarwal.

A-7. "Threat in the High Seas" by *Tehelka* dated 23.9.2006.

A-8. Confidential Report dated 27.9.2004 of Integrated Headquarters of Ministry of Defence (Navy), "Activities at ship-breaking yard, Alang."

A-9. Letter of Tom Haugen dated 19.07.2007 to the Chairman of Technical Experts Committee.

A-10. Report of the Committee of Atomic Energy Regulatory Board (AERB) dated 14.08.2007.

A-11. Excerpts from the Order dated 14.10.2003 of the Supreme Court of India.

A-12. Order dated 11.9.2007 of the Supreme Court of India.

A-13. Excerpts of Judgment dated 06.07.2012 of the Supreme Court of India.

A - 1

R209 – Bill of Sale – Version 1.1

Entered this 19 day of January 2006
at 7:35 am/pm
Registrar of Bahamian Ships
London:

THE COMMONWEALTH OF THE BAHAMAS

BILL OF SALE

Official Number	IMO Number	Name of Ship	Port of Registry
710763	5119143	SS NORWAY	NASSAU

Propulsion and Engine Details (given without warranty)	Vessel Dimensions
Propulsion: Two single geared turbines (damaged)	Length: 291.3 metres
Type of Engines: Steam two CEM Parsons (damaged)	Breadth: 33.7 metres
Total Power: 30,000 kW @125rpm (not warranted)	Depth: 15.8 metres

Particulars of Tonnage

GROSS TONNAGE: 76,049 tons

NET TONNAGE: 45,886 tons

We Norwegian Cruise Line Limited, of Milner House 18 Parliament Street, Hamilton, Bermuda (hereinafter called the "Transferor"), in consideration of the sum of US$10.00 (in words, Ten United States Dollars) and other good and valuable consideration paid to us by Bridgend Shipping Limited, of 80 Broad Street, Monrovia, Liberia (hereinafter called the "Transferee") the receipt of which is hereby acknowledged, hereby transfer to the Transferee 64/64 shares in the ship described above, and in its boats and appurtenances in accordance with and subject to the terms, conditions, exceptions and exclusions contained in the DEMOLISHCON Contract dated 1 January 2006 and made between the Transferor as seller and the Transferee as buyer of the ship described above. Further, the Transferor hereby covenants with the Transferee that the Transferor has power to transfer in the manner aforesaid, the premises hereinbefore expressed to be transferred and that the same are free from cluters, mortgages, encumbrances, maritime lieos and any other debts.

In witness whereof this Bill of Sale has been executed and delivered as a deed at London, England on the 16* day of January 2006.

Seal	Individual/Corporation	Attestation
	Norwegian Cruise Line Limited name of individual/corporation per PA Turner PAUL ALAN TURNER signature as Individual/Director/Secretary/Officer/Attorney-in-fact signature as Individual/Director/Secretary/Officer/Attorney-in-fact in the presence of the witness whose attestation is given opposite. R.A. Smith Notary Public London, England (Richard J. Saville)	I, (c) .... of (f) .... hereby testify that in my presence (i) this Bill of Sale was signed by .... as Individual/Director/Secretary/Officer/Attorney-in-fact (g) and .... as Individual/Director/Secretary/Officer/Attorney-in-fact (g) and .... (ii) the corporate seal/personal seal (g) of .... the transferor was affixed this ...... day of .... Signature of witness ....

Notes:

1. If the transferor is a body corporate the Bill of Sale should be carried on behalf of the body corporate by one or more directors/officers of the body corporate authorised for this purpose (as required by its constitution and under the seal of the body corporate (if it has a seal) or by duly authorised Attorney-in-fact.
2. The expression "Transferor" and "Transferee" used in this document shall include all heirs, successors, assigns, executors and administrators or any other legal representative.
3. Registered owners are reminded of the importance of keeping the Registrar of Bahamian Ships informed of any change of residence or registered office on their part.
4. The witness to the execution of the document must be a disinterested party, independent of the body corporate or individual executing it e.g. Consular Officer, Magistrate, Justice of Peace, Notary Public. A director, officer or employee of a Transferor which is a body corporate should not be an attesting witness.

(a) Insert the full name and address of each registered owner (Transferor)
(b) Insert the full name and address of each Transferee. Where there is more than one Transferee, the Transferees are joint owners.
(c) Insert the number of shares.
(d) If any subsisting encumbrance add "*save as appears by the registry of the said ship*".
(e) Insert name of witness, see note 4.
(f) Insert address of witness.
(g) Delete as appropriate.

PAT

REGISTRAR OF BAHAMIAN SHIPS
19 JAN 2006
LONDON ENGLAND

Government of Peoples Republic of Bangladesh

Ministry of Environment and Forest

Branch-7
No. pabama/sha-6/paper cliping-2/2005/51

Subject: Regarding Entry of Carrier of Hazardous Materials SS Norway

1. With reference to the above subject it is noted that being attracted by the news item titled "Floating SS Norway- the carrier of hazardous material is proceeding towards Bangladesh for scrapping", the environmentalists and others protested the entry of the ship into Bangladesh and in that backdrop an inter-ministerial meeting was held on 15-02-06 at the Ministry of Environment and Forest. The meeting took the following decisions. The Hon'ble Minister for Environment and Forest has approved the decisions:
   (a) The Bangladesh Bank shall be requested to give necessary directions to the commercial banks not to open L/C to import the ship called SS Norway.
   (b) The Navy, Chittagong Port Authority and the Coast Guard Authority shall be requested to take necessary steps not to allow the entry of the ship into Bangladesh.
   (c) National Board of Revenue shall be requested to take necessary measures regarding non-entry of the ship into Bangladesh.
2. According to the Basel Convention, ILO Convention and the rules of WTO signatory countries have the right to refuse any material or carrier that can cause harm to the environment Section 6 (a) of the Environment Conservation Act, 1995 has this provision.
3. In the circumstances stated, it is being requested under instruction to take necessary measures to ensure that the ship SS Norway (even if it has changed the name) does not enter Bangladesh.

Tahmina Akhter
Senior Assistant Secretary
Phone 7162072

Copy:

1. The Governor, Bangladesh Bank, Main Office, Dhaka
2. The Chief of Navy, Navy Head Office, Banani, Dhaka
3. The Secretary, Ministry of Home Affairs, Bangladesh Secretariat, Dhaka
4. The Chairman, National Board of Revenue, Segenbagicha, Dhaka
5. The Chairman, Chittagong Port Authority, Chittagong
6. The Director, Coast Guard, Head Office, DOHS, Baridhara, Dhaka-1206

Copy to necessary information:

1. PS to the Hon'ble Minister, Ministry of Environment and Forest
2. PS to the Hon'ble State Minister, Ministry of Environment and Forest
3. PS to the Secretary, Ministry of Environment and Forest
4. The Joint Secretary (Development) Ministry of Environment and Forest
5. The Joint Secretary (Environment) Ministry of Environment and Forest.

TRANSLATION

Peninsular Malaysia Marine Department
Marine Head Office
P.O.Box No. 12, Jalan Limbungan
42007 Port Klang
Selangor Darul Ehsan
Malaysia

Tel	: 03 – 3346 7777	Email	: kpgr@marine.gov.my
Fax	: 03 – 3168 5289	Web address	: www.marine.gov.my

Your Ref:
Our Ref: (47) dlm.IPL. 1845 – A Jld.3

Date: 19 May 2006

President,
Consumers Association of Penang,
10, Jalan Masjid Negeri,
11600 Penang.

Dear Sir

SS NORWAY DOCKED IN MALAYSIAN WATERS

Respectfully, I have been instructed to refer to the above matter and to your letter, Ref No. CAP/RS/Sg/SSNrwy/06/Mgs dated 05 May 2006.

2. Please be informed that SS Norway left Malaysian waters for Dubai on 05 May 2005 at 3.00pm. We were informed that the said ship was on its way to Dubai for repair works.

Thank you.

"SERVING THE NATION"

By the order of,

-sgd-
(Md Badron Bin Ismail)
Safety of Navigation Division
f. Director General of Marine,
Peninsular Malaysia

33 2006
K/L KANNAN
Tamil,
Inggi,
Pulau Pinang.

'Blue Lady is now India's problem'

Times of India

Nitin Sethi | TNN

New Delhi: Gujarat Pollution Control Board, in its affidavit before the SC, has claimed that the controversial *Blue Lady* ship cannot now be removed from Indian shores.

It will have to be broken down at Alang, Gujarat, the board has said in the affidavit in the on-going case of alleged illegal beaching of the vessel in India. The board has said in its report that the 'dismantling plan submitted by the recycler may be accepted' under certain conditions.

The petitioners had filed an application in the apex court in May 2006 asking the court to ensure that the ship complied with international law, national law and the court's own order of October 2003 before its arrival at the Indian port, alleging that it contained illegal hazardous material. The petition had asked for disallowing beaching of the ship till the court adjudicated.

However, in June the court had permitted *Blue Lady* to anchor at Alang on humanitarian grounds on the basis of an interim report of the technical committee on ship-breaking, chaired by Prodipto Ghosh, secretary of the ministry of environment and forests. The technical committee had cited two reasons. One, that monsoons were approaching and if the ship was not anchored, then it may get damaged, and two, that there were 13 Indians on board lacking adequate food.

Now the Gujarat Pollution Control Board, after considering the recycling and dismantling management plan and the technical committee report, has told the court that "any effort to pull back the vessel can result to capsize (sic), resulting in becoming a wreck" and that "a beached ship cannot usually be refloated".

TROUBLE-MAKER

The implications of the affidavit would be that regardless of the legality of the ship, the country is now saddled with the controversial vessel. "There are two versions of the technical committee report, one claiming that there is hazardous waste on board and another saying there is none," said Gopal Krishna, the petitioner.

Khaleej Times ONLINE

Did mystery ship owners lie over fate of ssNorway?

A Khaleej Times Scrutiny Exclusive

30 June 2006

DOCUMENTS obtained by enviornmental campaigners appear to show the present owners of the ssNorway, the famous cruise liner Dubai investors want to save from an Indian ship breaking yard, gave false information to marine, government and court officials.

The ship, now renamed the 'Blue Lady,' is considered the last of the great cruise ships and to be of great cultural significance in the annals of maritime history. The vessel has been bought by a consortium of Indian scrappers who plan to tear the 1000-foot liner apart for her steel.

The ship is currently owned by a mysterious Liberian shell company, Bridgeend Shipping, who apparently bought the ship from its long-time owners and operators, the Malaysian-based Star Cruises. Bridgeend, in turn, is holding a promissory note for $19.3 million from the consortium of Indian breakars, Haryana Steel, in payment for the liner.

The true owners or controllers of Bridgeend Shipping is not known, although sources have told Khaeej Times the company has an interest in Haryana Steel.

The scrapping is being vigorously opposed by environmental groups who say the Indian breakers do not have the facilities or technology to safely dispose of the estimated 1,000 tons of asbestos used as fire retardent on board the ship. Last month, the Indian Supreme Court ordered a special Technical Committee to inspect the Blue Lady and assess the asbestos risk before she is allowed to be scrapped. The ship has been granted permission to anchor in Indian waters while the court makes its decision.

The Khaleej Times has learnt the Blue Lady was due to drop anchor at Alang at 8.40am Friday. Once there, she will be boarded by the inspection team, who are already in the town investigating the ability of the scrapper to safely dispose of the asbestos. Their report is expected by the end of the first week of July.

Yesterday, however, the Khaleej Times obtained access to documents that reveal the ship's owners gave apparently misleading information to marine and government officials in order to move the ship from its former berth at Kalang Harbor, Malaysia to India.

According to a document provided by the Malaysian Maritime Department, Bridgeend Shipping told Malay authorities on May 19 they were sailing to Dubai where the Blue Lady was to undergo 'repairs'.

In fact, the liner was towed directly to India. Once there, the ship's owners appealed to the Supreme Court to be allowed to anchor in Indian Waters on 'humanitarian grounds'. On June 5, a month after leaving Malaysia, the owners claimed the Indian crew would not be safe on the boat during monsoon season and might run out of food and water. In response, the court allowed the liner to anchor, but only until the technical Committee report was complete.

Then, the liner was turned around and towed to the UAE, docking at Fujairah for two days before again being towed back to the edge of Indian territorial waters.

Gopal Krishna, who is coordinating the environment campaign to prevent the ship being scrapped in India, said by misrepresenting the true destination of the Blue Lady when she left Malaysia, Bridgeebd Shipping had violated international law.

Specifically, he said, the owners had violated the United Nations Basel Convention on Hazardous Wastes which stipulates that ships containing material such as asbestos must be decontaminated in the home country first before being broken up.

Mr Krishna said the ship left Kalang having already been sold for scrapping by the Liberian shell company. Therefore the ship should have been cleared of asbestos in Liberia. Instead the owners appear to have moved the vessel on the notion it was being repaired in the UAE, when in fact it was going to India for scrapping.

Mr Krishna said: "Additionally, they told the court they needed to anchor in Indian waters on humanitarian grounds because the crew might be at risk. Why then did they, after they were granted permission, move the ship to UAE and then bring her back again? If they were really concerned about crew safety, would they have not immediately moved her directly into Indian waters or, having moved her to the UAE, kept her docked there until the monsoons were over?"

Mr Krishna said he would be filing the documents with the Supreme Court as part of the case opposing the ship's destruction in India.

In the meantime, there is growing support for 'Project Dubai', a $120 million rescue plan developed by a joint UAE/US consortium of investors to save the ship and bring it to Dubai as a floating hotel, conference,

restaurant and cultural center. Since the Khaleej Times story of June 28, Project Dubai's investors have been flooded with calls and offers of support.

John Voet, one of Project Dubai's US partners, said they were committed to having the Blue Lady's asbestos expertly removed and made safe before she was brought back to the UAE. "The risk from the asbestos is only a risk if the ship is broken up,' he said. "We want to make sure everyone walks away from this happy."

Rashid al Noori, a UAE partner, said: "The ship is still beautiful - a work of art. She needs cleaning and some attention, but there is no doubt she could become exactly the kind of niche project envisioned by

His Highness Shaikh Mohammad bin Rashid Al Maktoum to bring the cultures of other nations into Dubai."

PROF. M.G.K. MENON

K-5, Hauz Khas Enclave

New Delhi-110016

Tel No. 011-26511454

August 14, 2006

Dear Hon'ble Chief Justice of India Shri Y.K. Sabharwal,

I am writing this in my capacity as former Chairman of the High Powered Committee on Management of Hazardous Wastes appointed at the instance of the Supreme Court of India. The Report of this Committee had been fully accepted by the Supreme Court in the Judgment dated 14.10.2003.

I am writing this concerning recent events relating to a Maritime Liner *SS Blue Lady* (Ex. SS Norway, SS France). I am given to understand that the Gujarat Pollution Control Board as also a Technical Committee has recommended that the Vessel be beached in India, and that the Supreme Court had accepted this recommendation on humanitarian grounds relating to individuals on board.

I wish to draw you attention to fact that *SS Blue Lady* belongs to Star Cruises of Malaysia. It is their responsibility and that of the Government of Malaysia to ensure that the Ship is either reconditioned as a Maritime Liner, or ensure environmentally sound disposal - as the French Government did in the case of Aircraft Carrier "Le Clemenceau".

The orders of the Supreme Court dated 14th October, 2003 clearly state:

"Ship Breaking

We accept the following recommendations of HPC

"1. Before a ship arrives at port it should have proper consent from the concerned authority on the State Maritime Board, stating that it does not contain any hazardous waste or radioactive substances AERB should be consulted in the matter in appropriate cases.

"2. The ship should be properly decontaminated by the ship owner prior to the breaking. This should be ensured by the SPCBs".

In my view, there should be no violation of these orders. Even if the vessel is beached it should only be on a temporary basis, (for the humanitarian reasons that have been advanced) until it can be returned to Malaysia. If the idea is to transfer it to India's possession, it should either be retired as an ocean liner which has had a great history, or decontaminated before ship-breaking is undertaken. Any effort to dilute the Supreme Court orders of October 14, 2003, or try to remove the concept of prior decontamination would be a measure going against the interests of workers in the ship-breaking yards as also a violation of the Basel Convention. This will be a violation by both Malaysia and India who are signatories to the Convention.

I am writing this letter to you in a personal capacity as someone who is interested as a citizen of the country and as a scientist in the field who would like to see proper observance of environmental norms.

With warm regards,

Yours sincerely,
(M.G.K. Menon)

Hon'ble Shri Y.K. Sabharwal
Chief Justice of India,
Supreme Court of India,
Tilak Marg,
New Delhi-110001

23/09/2006

Tehelka

THREAT IN THE HIGH SEAS

Terror's Trojan horse docks at Alang, says Navy report

No checks on vessels like the Blue Lady and the Clemenceau may mean that they could carry contraband, bombs, says a naval intelligence report

Sanjay Dubey
New Delhi :

Along with the asbestos and other harmful material, decommissioned ships cart grave security risks to Alang, the world's largest shipbreaking yard in Gujarat.

Tehelka is in possession of a onfidential report prepared by the Directorate of Naval Intelligence in late 2004, which draws attention to how "some ships arriving at the breaking yards may not actually undergo the (dismantling) process, but disappear from anchorage, after a short duration, to unknown destinations". There is a likelihood, the report suggests, "that such ships may be involved in nefarious activities" and, while it clarifies that "no known case of landing of contraband and explosives has come to light", it also says that "the involvement of Pak nationals/Dawood gang makes it a distinct possibility". Noting that it is common for ships not to undergo security checks until they have permission to beach, the report warns: "Since the vessel is bound for shipbreaking, it has genuine cover to anchor everywhere for emergency repairs. This would afford ample opportunity to the crew to indulge in activities detrimental to our security." The report lists dumping of radioactive material in Indian waters under the guise of shipbreaking, using ships as drop-point for spies and the possibility of clandestine surveys of seabed and coastal areas and weather and meteorological data. None of these, the report says, can be ruled out.

The report was sent not only to the ministry of defence but also to the country's key intelligence agencies

The confidential report was sent not only to the ministry of defence (MoD), but also to the intelligence agencies with the caution that the issues raised were crucial and if unchecked could jeopardise India's maritime security. Auditing the records of the past two years, it is evident that these warnings have not only gone unheeded, they have in fact been utterly forgotten.

India, activists say, is already the world's biggest dumping ground for soon-to-be or already decommissioned ships. Facilitating the entry of potentially harmful decommissioned ships is a total disregar of laws governing the ships' trans-boundary movement. "Right from the Basel Convention and the Stockholm Convention for managing the international traffic of hazardous waste to the 2003 Supreme Cour order and the Central Pollution Control Board (CPCB) and International Maritime Organisation's (IMO) guidelines, all are flouted," says environmental activist Gopal Krishna. Typifying environmentalists' concern is Norwegian liner Blue Lady which is beached at Alang.

7 Sep 2004

INTEGRATED HEADQUARTERS OF MINISTRY OF DEFENCE (NAVY)

(Directorate of Naval Intelligence)

ACTIVITIES AT SHIP BREAKING YARD ALANG

1. An incident having serious security implications has come to light wherein a Dead Bulk Carrier S Araz was towed to Alang by Russian Tug Kapitan Maryshkin for ship breaking. The vessel was boarded by Customs and other authorities on 20 May 04 for requisite clearance. It has been reported that the vessel subsequently stayed off Alang with the Tug and then sailed off without any information on 27 May 04.

2. This incident has clearly brought out the security lacunae at Alang, wherein some ship arriving at the breaking yards may not actually undergo the process but disappear from anchorage after a short duration, to unknown destinations. There is also a possibility that such ships may be involved in nefarious activities. During preliminary investigations, it has emerged that the departure of such vessels from anchorage without intimation is a common practice.

3. The above incident was investigated further with a view to streamline the existing procedures of accountability of ships arriving at breaking yards. Some of the areas of concern that have emerged are enumerated in succeeding paragraphs.

Security Concerns

4. The high stakes of profit margin, cheap labour, corrupt practices and a large fleeting population has made labour settlement in Alang an ideal breeding ground for Mafia and anti-national elements to indulge in nefarious activities, almost unhindered.

Financial

5. The Cash Buyers operate hand in glove with the End buyers and owners, by under-invoicing the deal. The unmentioned amount transacted through the Hawala route making almost 40 to 50% metal trade illegal.

Involvement of Pak National / Dawood Gang

6. Apparently, a Huge number of Cash Buyers are Pak additional based at London/UAE. Due to large profit margins, Dawood Group appears to have invested heavily in Cash Buyer thus having a stake in most deals.

Smuggling off Contraband/Explosives/Agents.

7. Though no known case of landing of contraband and explosives has come to light, the involvement of Pak nationals/Dawood gang makes it a distinct possibility.

Environmental/Security Check

8. Due laxity and non-availability of requisite infrastructure with Gujarat Pollution Control Board (GPCB), the possibility of offloading of hazardous material including, radio-active waste on Indian shores under the guise of ship breaking activity is a distinct possibility.

Vessels Stopping at Other Routs Enroute Alang

9. It has come to light that the last port call of some vessels bound for Alang could be adjusted to give them a right of innocent passage through any portion of Indian waters. Since the vessel is bound for ship breaking, it has a genuine cover to anchor anywhere for emergency repairs. This would afford ample opportunity to the crew to Indulge in activities detrimental to our security if so desired by them.

Unscrupulous Activities

10. The crew of the vessels coming in Alang under own power go through the security checks viz. Immigration, Customs etc. provided the ship is finally accepted for beaching. However, if the deals fall through, the crew goes back unchecked. Thus possibility of breaking off the deal intentionally after a stay of four-five days at Alang outer anchorage cannot be ruled out. This also applies to the dead vessels, which are towed by tugs/another vessels. The escorting vessel stays with the dead vessel till final permission for latter's beaching is accorded. Since the escorting vessel has the status of a vessel on innocent passage through territorial waters of India, the crew and the vessel in itself escape scrutiny. Due to the extended unchecked stay the possibility of using this method for clandestine SIGINT collection, survey of seabed and coastal area, weather and meteorological data and for dropping/picking of agents cannot be ruled out.

Recommendations

11. The above issues have a wider ramification and need to be watched by our Intelligence Agencies, R&AW and IB have, therefore, been informed accordingly. MOD will also appreciate that the above issues are crucial and, if allowed to go unchecked can jeopardise our maritime security. In view of the above, following is strongly recommended:

    (a) Prior MOD clearance for all such vessels by the purchaser through Alang Port Authorities be made mandatory at the earliest.

    (b) Regular boarding/security check by the Coast Guard and Port Authorities of ship-breaking vessels at outer anchorage is required to be put into force. MOD may accordingly take up the issue with the Government of Gujarat.

12. The above issues, if correctly addressed, would ensure that appropriate measures are instituted to safeguard India's Maritime Security, its environment and economy appropriately.

(UK Thapa)
Commander
JDNI-4

Shri HG Syal
Under Secretary (Ops))
D/(N-II/Opp)
Ministry of Defence

PROJECT MANAGEMENT INSTALLATION SS NORWAY FIRE DETECTION SYSTEM INSTALLATION SS NORWAY

Tom Haugen tell: +47 91384454 E-mail: tom@ultratech.no
Tech no.
Faret 4
N-1560 Larkollen
Norway

To,
Chairman, Committee of Technical Experts (CTE)

Att: Mrs. Meena Gupta
CC: Mr. Gopal Krishna

Date: July 19, 2007

Subject: Fire detection system installation S/S Norway

This letter is a statement and explanation for the fire detection installation onboard SS Norway, Ex. SS France which clarify original installation from 1960, new installation (complete new) in 1980 and latest upgrades in 1990's. This statement is also a concern for how the system installation with our radioactive detectors shall be handled and destructed.

My involvement with SS Norway, has been as a project manager for engineering, delivery, installation, commissioning and later services and upgrades onboard from 1990, as employed by the manufacture. Autronica Fire and Security AS, Trondheim, Norway.

In 1990 Kloster Cruise/ NCL decided to do an upgrade for the existing fire detection system, installed in 1980 when the vessel was under reconstruction in Germany. The 1980 installation was done by a Norwegian company named Signalco AS under management of Mr. Kjell Stein (Died in 1996/7). Mr.Stein was employed by Autronica from 1987 and was my colleague when the upgrade of the fire detection system took place from 1990. We worked in the team and because of Mr. Steins knowledge of the vessel's existing fire detection system it was of most importance to know all details, also for the first installed fire detection system from 1960.

From one of our first pre-survey, our aim was to specify all details related to existing system installation which was important for engineering and design of the new system installation of Autronica BS-100 as an addressable system in replacement for Signalco conventional system installation. This pre-survey included specifications of the first installation from 1960 as the original detection system. The original central unit system was installed and kept unchanged in the vessel's safety room together with other original systems related to the safety equipment installation from 1960's. The original fire detection system installation was done with that times most advanced equipment and to keep the system in operation also during a fire, the loop installation was done with copper mantled and properly asbestos filled cables, named "Pyotenax". Detectors was from it's original installed in high fire risk areas and public spaces and was of lone detectors, which means a source with radioactive sensor, Americium 241. This installation was kept unchanged because the new fire detection system from 1980 needed complete new loop cables and was independent of original installation from 1960, also due to the fact that the existing cables could not be used. Original smoke detectors are then remaining onboard but not knowing in details the total numbers of detectors. As long as the "new" installation from 1980 required complete new centrals (on bridge this time) and cables for the loop system, the original detector system was kept unchanged, but disconnected from the vessel's alarm and detection system. These detectors will be found behind ceilings and other places which were reconstructed back in 1980.

The new fire detection system with Autronica BS-100, installed in 1990's. was designed with approximately 5500 detection points and have 1100 of radioactive elements, Americiun, 241.

All sensors connected to the installed system from 1980 was replaced with Autronica smoke detectors, all loop cabling used and remaining, existing /old detectors from Signalco product was then destructed.

From me and all partners within fire detection system equipment deliveries, we are very concerned for any removing / dismantling of all installed radioactive detectors from its original back in 1960 and the new system installation.

Importance:

Removing or handling of radio active sensors with "Americium 241" element has to be done by skilled persons, knowing exactly what to do and for any circumstances, non un-expert handling. All detectors have to be destructed in a safe way, which means by certified laboratories which are approved by the government

For any projects which include removing old radioactive detector, we are demanded to contract the legal way of destruction, with return of signed statement for the total numbers shipped and received for destruction to any certified laboratory, signed by the authorised company for removal.

Any other solutions or behaviour will have human dangers risk for non-skilled persons and environmental dumping. One detector itself will not harm any, but a total number of 1100+ will defiantly be a high risk if handling without expertise and right procedures.

Best regards

Tom Haugen

Project manager fire detection systems

Tel: +47 91384454

Emai: ltom@ultra-te

REPORT ON THE INSPECTION OF BLUE LADY SHIP BENCHED AT ALANG-SOSIYA SHIP RECYCLING YARD

Introduction:

MV *Blue Lady* ship, which was beached on August 16, 2006 is under sub-judice for her breaking because of the litigation filed in the Hon'ble Supreme Court by one advocate. In view of this, and in the light of the content of the affidavit filed by the said petitioner, Gujarat Maritime Board (GMB), Gandhinagar requested the Chairman, Atomic Energy Regulatory Board (ABRB), Mumbai to inspect the said ship for the detection of presence if any radioactive material in the ship. AERB deputed Mr R K Singh, Scientific Officer (E), AERB, for the inspection of the ship along with the BARC trained personnel from GMB. The personnel from GMB are 1) Mr M M Parmar, Safety Supervisor, RSO-1, GMB, Alang and 2) Miss Dina Patel-Environment Cell, GMB, RSO-1, Gandhinagar.

About the *Blue Lady*

Blue Lady was a passenger ship constructed in 1952 and initially originated from France and the last origin was from Norway and her earlier name was S S NORWAY. The Ship has about 291mt length and 34mt width and 45886 MT capacity. The above information were gathered from the ship breaker.

The ship also has 16 numbers of docks (floors). The top flour (16th deck) is the terrace and the 15th deck has one basketball ground. There are two swimming pools and one open restaurant on the 14th floor. The ship has more than 1401 cabins (rooms) for passenger accommodation and some fully furnished and well- decorated VVIP rooms. In addition to the above, the ship has also one in-house restaurant, one mini-theatre, one spacious heath club and one duty free shopping complex. Up to 6th floor of the ship, it was mainly for use by the passengers and the engine decks start from bottom and are up to 5th floor.

Inspection:

The team comprising of personnel from AERB and GMB arrived at the premise of M/s Priya Blue Industries Pvt Ltd, Plot No. V-1, Sosiya Ship Recycling Yard (the present owner of the ship) at around 14:30 hrs on 14th August 2007. The team had to wait for about one hour for tide, so they can reach to the ship (away about 3500 ft from the shore) for the inspection. While we were waiting for the tide, we discussed about the ship with the ship breaker company officials and gathered some prime information about the ship. The Govt officials were accompanied by one official from the ship breaker. It was a cloudy and light rainy day and the sea was also rough and choppy. However, looking at the limited time available for the inspection due to tide time, we started the boat ride at 15:15 hrs and reached at the ship at around 16:00 hrs. It was not an easy exercise for all of us to get into the ship using that rope-ladder hanging from the ship at a height above 25 feet and one end of the ladder attached to the boat swinging due to the strong sea current. We reached, first, at fifth floor and started inspection from the terrace (16th floor) downwards. Each floor has two passages (Gangways) and rooms are on both side of each gangway. Each cabin (room) is fitted with at least two nos of smoke detectors and smoke detectors are also fitted along the passages. However, these smoke detectors are all optical based (Photo-electric) detector. But, we could locate some ionisation smoke detectors fitted in high voltage rooms, storage rooms, mechanical workshop room and system control (air-conditioning, cooling, oil and water pipelines) rooms. All these ionisation-based smoke detectors located were removed by us and verified that all these detectors had Am-241 sources of 0.9 MCi each, We could collect 12 nos of such smoke detectors and handed over to the breaker for keeping safely and securely pending their safe disposal at BARC through AERB, Mumbai. When we inspected the bottom of the ship (part of engine room areas). we found a particular area earmarked as EMERGENCY RESPONSE SERVICE. We could find there INSTRUCTIONS written on the board to be followed during emergency response for the hazardous materials present in the ship. However, we could not find any instructions for emergency response related with radioactive material. Also we could not find any radioactive warning symbol in any part of the ship except in the ionisation-based smoke detectors. In addition to this, the inventory of the hazardous material issued by the Master of the ship does not mention anything about the radioactive material. With this, we completed the inspection of the ship at around 20:00 hrs and returned backed to the shore at 21:00 hrs.

Conclusion:

Based on the findings obtained during the inspection of the ship carried out by the officials of AERB, Mumbai and GMB, it is concluded that the ship M V *Blue Lady* presently benched in Plot No. V-1, Sosiya Ship Recycling Yard). Now, does not contain any radioactive material on board the ship.

(R K Singh) (M M Parmar) (Dina P Patel)

IN THE SUPREME COURT OF INDIA
WRIT PETITION NO. 657 OF 1995

Research Foundation for Science Technology National Resource Policy **Appellant(s)**

Versus

Union of India & Others **Respondent (s)**

(With SLP (C) No. 16175/1997 & C.A. No. 7660/1997)

ORDER DATED 14.10.2003

1. Hazardous Wastes are highly toxic in nature. The industrialization has had the effect of generation of huge quantities of hazardous wastes. These and other side effects of development gave birth to principles of sustainable development so as to sustain industrial growth. The hazardous waste required adequate and proper control and handling. Efforts are required to be made to minimise it. In developing nations, there are additional problems including that of dumping of hazardous waste on their lands by some of the nations where cost of destruction of such waste is felt very heavy. These and other allied problems gave birth to Basel Convention. The key objectives of the Basel Convention are :

   "to minimize the generation of hazardous wastes in terms of quantity and hazardousness;to dispose of them as close to the source of generation as possible;to reduce the transboundary movement of hazardous wastes."

2. Due to alarming situation created by dumping of hazardous waste, its generation and serious and irreversible damage, as a result thereof, to the environment, flora and fauna, health of animals and human beings, the petitioner approached this Court under Article 32 complaining of violation of Article 14 and 21 of the Constitution of India.

3. The petitioner has, inter alia, relied upon the Basel Convention. The Basel Convention was signed by India on 15th March, 1990 and ratified on 24th June, 1992.

4. From time to time various affidavits have been filed in this matter by

Ministry of Environment and Forests (for short MoEF) and Pollution Control Boards. The aspects that have been considered and reflected in various orders that have been passed and are further required to be considered and appropriate directions issued relate to the provisions of Hazardous Waste (Management and Handling) Rules, 1989 (for short H.W. Rules), the implementation of these Rules and other connected issues relating to hazardous waste. These Rules have been amended during pendency of this petition, the latest amendment being of 23rd May, 2003.

5. Considering the magnitude of the problem and the extent of hazardous waste generated, this Court issued notices to all the State Governments, Central Pollution Control Board and State Pollution Control Boards so as to identify the problem, identify the extent of such waste, availability of the disposal sites and various other aspects relevant to minimising the generation, its proper handling and disposal with a view to safeguard the environment degradation.

6. By order dated 5th May, 1997, this Court, inter alia, directed that no authorisation/permission would be given by any authority for the import of hazardous waste items which have already been banned by the Central Government or by any order made by any Court or any other authority and no import would be made or permitted by any authority or any person, of any hazardous waste which is already banned under the Basel Convention or to be banned hereafter with effect from the dates specified therein. In view of the magnitude of the problem and its impact, the State Governments were directed to show cause why an order be not made directing closure of units utilising the hazardous waste where provision is not already made for requisite safe disposal sites. It was further ordered that cause be shown as to why immediate order be not made for closure of all unauthorised hazardous waste handling units.

7. We have extensively perused the record with the assistance of learned counsel. The material on record demonstrates that proper attention was not paid by the concerned authorities in implementing H.W. Rules, 1989. These Rules were amended with effect from 6th June, 2000 and further amended on 23rd May, 2003. The problem is not as much of absence of the Rules as it is of implementation. If the Rules are amended, but not implemented the same remain on paper. If H.W. rules as in 1989 had been properly implemented, the problem would not have been as grave

as faced now. Likewise, if the Rules as amended in the year 2000 were implemented, the problem would not have been as grave as it is presently.

8. Our attention has been drawn by Mr. Parikh, learned counsel for the petitioner, to various orders that have been passed by this Court commencing from 19th October, 1995 till date, to various affidavits that have been filed on behalf of the MOEF, Central Pollution Control Board (CPCB) and others which substantially amount to an admission of the authorities about lack of various basics so as to handle the issue. One of the such elementary aspect is lack of correct information as to the extent of the hazardous wastes. At one stage it was represented that the total quantity of hazardous wastes generated in the Country was in the region of 2000 tonnes per day which worked out to be 0.7 million tonnes per year. At a later stage the figure rose to more than 4.4 million tonnes per year. This is just one illustration.

9. In the order dated 4th August, 1997 it was observed that all State Governments have not taken steps required under the applicable laws as well as earlier directions of the Court and have not placed before the Court all material facts inspite of considerable time having been given. It has been further observed that all the authorities do not appear to appreciate the gravity of situation and need for prompt measures being taken to prevent serious adverse consequences. Even Central Government was not given full information by all the State Governments about the compliance of the directions of this Court. Under these circumstances, it was observed that an appropriate Committee deserves to be constituted to ensure that needful is done to arrest further growth of the problem. Learned counsel for the petitioner and the learned Additional Solicitor General were requested to furnish the names of suitable persons including experts who could be appointed to such Committee. In this background, by order dated 13th October, 1997 a High Powered Committee (HPC) with Prof. MGK. Menon as its Chairman was constituted to examine all matters in depth relating to hazardous waste and to give a report and recommendations at an early date. The fourteen Terms of Reference on which the High Powered Committee was required to give its report and recommendations are :

(1) Whether and to what extent the hazardous wastes listed in Basel Convention have been banned by the Govt. and to examine which other hazardous wastes, other than listed in Basel Convention

and Hazardous Wastes (Management and Handling) Rules, 1989, require banning.

(2) To verify the present status of the units handling hazardous wastes imported for recycling or generating/recycling indigenous hazardous wastes on the basis of information provided by respective States/UTs and determine the status of implementation of Hazardous Wastes (Management and Handling) Rules, 1989 by various States/UTs and in the light of directions issued by the Hon'ble Supreme Court.

(3) What safeguards have been put in place to ensure that banned toxic/ hazardous wastes are not allowed to be imported.

(4) What are the changes required in the existing laws to regulate the functioning of units handling hazardous wastes and for protecting the people (including workers in the factory) from environmental hazards.

(5) To assess the adequacy of the existing facilities for disposal of hazardous wastes in an environmentally sound manner and to make recommendations about the most suitable manner for disposal of hazardous wastes.

(6) What is further required to be done to effectively prohibit, monitor and regulate the functioning of units handling hazardous wastes keeping in view the existing body of laws.

(7) To make recommendations as to what should be the prerequisites for issuance of authorisation/permission under Rule 5 and Rule 11 of the Hazardous Wastes (Management and Handling) Rules, 1989.

(8) To identify the criteria for designation of areas for locating units handling hazardous wastes and waste disposal sites.

(9) To determine as to whether the authorisation/permissions given by the State Boards for handling hazardous wastes are in accordance with Rule 5(4) and Rule 11 of hazardous waste Rules, 1989 and whether the decision of the State Pollution Control Boards is based on any prescribed procedure of checklist.

(10) To recommend a mechanism for publication of inventory at regular intervals giving area-wise information about the level and nature of hazardous wastes.

(11) What should be the framework for reducing risks to environment and public health by stronger regulation and by promoting production methods and products which are ecologically friendly and thus reduce the production of toxics?

(12) To consider any other related area as the Committee may deem fit.

(13) To examine the quantum and nature of hazardous waste stock lying at the docks/ports/ICDs and recommend a mechanism for its safe disposal or re-export to the original exporters.

(14) Decontamination of ships before they are exported to India for breaking.

10. The High Powered Committee comprised of experts from different disciplines and fields as would be apparent from the following :-

1. Dr. Claude Alvares (scientific aspects of environmental damage and their impacts on society, legal aspects, Basel Convention, accountability to the public);
2. Dr. D.B. Boralkar (chemistry, pollution control, Basel Convention, experience at CPCB and SPCB in enforcement of regulations);
3. Dr. Mrs. Indrani Chandrasekharan (chemistry, formulation of legislation, Basel Convention, experience at MOEF);
4. Dr. V.K. Iya (chemistry and biomedical aspects, public involvement);
5. Shri Prem Chand (non-ferrous metals and industry);
6. Dr. K.R. Ranganathan (environmental studies, pollution control and functioning of CPCB, accountability to the public);
7. Dr. A.K. Saxena (environmental engineering, experience at National Productivity Council on hazardous waste management projects, particularly landfill technology);
8. Dr. P.K. Seth (aspects of health and hazardous wastes; industrial toxicology);
9. Dr. Sudhir Singhal (issues relating to oil);
10. Shri Paritosh Tyagi (pollution control, institutional mechanisms and experience as a former Chairman, CPCB);
11. Dr. R.R. Khan, Director, Ministry of Environment and Forests & Member-Secretary;
12. Dr. T.S.R. Prasad Rao, Director, Indian Institute of Petroleum, Dehra Dun (represented by Dr. Himmat Singh, Deputy Director).

11. With the assistance of Mr. Sanjay Parikh, learned counsel appearing for the petitioner, Mr. AND. Rao, learned counsel appearing for the Central Government and Mr. Vijay Panjwani learned counsel appearing for Central Pollution Control Board, we have gone through the extensive report submitted by High Powered Committee. At the outset, we wish to place on record our gratitude for the efforts made and dedication shown by HPC in preparation of the report and recommendations made therein after an indepth study of numerous facets of the problem.

12. The Report has highlighted the areas which result in generation of the hazardous wastes and the limited area on which the High Powered Committee focussed its attention, namely, industrial operations (solid, liquid, gaseous waste) including industries recycling hazardous waste and others as detailed in paragraph 1.3 relating to scope of work. Out of 14 Terms of Reference, on T.O.R.No. 13 the High Powered Committee submitted its Report on 20th April, 1998, on consideration whereof, directions were issued in terms of the order dated 10th December, 1999.

13. The ratification of Basel Convention by India shows the commitment of our country to solve the problem on the principles and basis stated in the said document. The decision stated to have been taken by 65 conference parties by consensus to ban all exports of hazardous wastes from Organisation for Economic Co-operation and Development (OECD) to non-OECD countries immediately for disposal and in the beginning of the year 1998 for recycling are, therefore, required to be kept in view while considering the number of items to be banned. It also deserved to be noticed that having regard to the broad outlook in framing the Terms of Reference including therein not only the aspects of imported hazardous wastes but also management of indigenous hazardous wastes, the HPC has rightly not confined itself just to the crisis situation that has arisen from continuous illegal import and dumping of hazardous wastes, but had also gone into the systemic weaknesses that had developed as a result whereof there was slow progress in handling the problem. HPC has observed that the problems raised by indigenous processing of toxic substances such as lead and waste oil and by industrial processes that generated these as also by methods of disposal like incinerators and landfills to be far more serious and of far greater magnitude than those associated with the import of such waste. In this view various aspects of indigenous generation and handling of hazardous wastes have been

examined in depth. Having regard to this approach, we agree with the conclusions drawn by HPC that MOEF made no concerted or consistent efforts which necessarily have to be of a promotional, educational and coordinating nature–to show the implementation of the HW Rules,1989. We hope that on the matter in issue, henceforth, there would not be any lack of serious and concerted action on the part of MoEF.

❑❑❑

15. First, the legal principles in brief may be noticed.

16. The legal position regarding applicability of the precautionary principle and polluter pays principle which are part of the concept of sustainable development in our country is now well settled. In Vellore Citizens' Welfare Forum vs. Union of India &Ors. [(1996) 5 SCC 647], a three Judge Bench of this Court, after referring to the principles evolved in various international conferences and to the concept of "sustainable development", inter alia, held that the precautionary principle and polluter pays principle have now emerged and govern the law in our country, as is clear from Articles 47, 48-A and 51-A(g) of our Constitution and that, in fact, in the various environmental statues including the Environment (Protection) Act, 1986, these concepts are already implied. These principles have been held to have become part of our law. Further, it was observed in *Vellore Citizens' Welfare Forum's case* that these principles are accepted as part of the customary international law and hence there should be no difficulty in accepting them as part of our domestic law. Reference may also be made to the decision in the case of *A.P. Pollution Control Board Vs. Prof. M.V. Nayudu (Retd.) and Ors.* [(1996 5 SCC 718] where, after referring to the principles noticed in Vellore Citizens' *Welfare Forum's Case*, the same have been explained in more detail with a view to enable the Courts and the Tribunals or environmental authorities to properly apply the said principles in the matters which come before them. In this decision, it has also been observed that the principle of good governance is an accepted principle of international and domestic laws. It comprises of the rule of law, effective State Institutions, transparency and accountability and public affairs, respect for human rights and the meaningful participation of citizens in the political process of their countries and in the decisions affecting their lives. Reference has also been made to Article 7 of the draft approved by the working group of the International Law Commission in 1996 on "Prevention

of Transboundary Damage from Hazardous Activities" to include the need for the State to take necessary legislative, administrative and other actions" to implement the duty of prevention of environmental harm. Environmental concerns have been placed at same pedestal as human rights concerns, both being traced to Article 21 of the Constitution of India. It is the duty of this Court to render justice by taking all aspects into consideration. It has also been observed that with a view to ensure that there is neither danger to the environment nor to the ecology and, at the same time, ensuring sustainable development, the Court can refer scientific and technical aspects for an investigation and opinion to expert bodies. The provisions of a covenant which elucidate and go to effectuate the fundamental rights guaranteed by our Constitution, can be relied upon by Courts as facets of those fundamental rights and hence enforceable as such (see People's Union for Civil Liberties Vs. Union of India &Anr. [(1997) 3 SCC 433]. *The Basel Convention, it cannot be doubted, effectuates the fundamental rights guaranteed under Article 21. The rights to information and community participation for protection of environment and human health is also a right which flows from Article 21. The Government and authorities have, thus to motivate the public participation. These well-shrined principles have been kept in view by us while examining and determining various aspect and facets of the problems in issue and the permissible remedies.*

❑❑❑

19. The Basel Convention, which we have noticed hereinbefore has banned import of 76 items. The H.W. Rules, 1989, however, ban 29 items. What is the position of the remaining items, we do not know except the stand of MOEF that the same is under consideration. We do wish to place on record that the Report of High Powered Committee (HPC) was submitted nearly 2 ½ years ago. Considering the magnitude of the problem the MOEF should have bestowed more serious consideration that it has on these matters and taken appropriate steps.

❑❑❑

37. Section 3(2)(12) of the Environment Protection Act, 1986 stipulates collection and dissemination of information in respect of matters relating to environmental pollution. Principle 10 of the Rio Declaration recognizes the right to receive information and community participation with particular emphasis on hazardous materials. The said principle reads as under :

"Principle 10: Environmental issues are best handled with the participation of all concerned citizens, at the relevant level. At the national level, each individual shall have appropriate access to information concerning the environment, that is held by public authorities, including information on hazardous materials and activities in their communities, and the opportunity to participate in decision making processes. States shall facilitate and encourage public awareness and participation by making information widely available. Effective access to judicial and administrative proceedings, including redress and remedy, shall be provided."

38. Principle 4 stipulates that in order to achieve sustainable development, environmental protection shall constitute an integral part of the development process and cannot be considered in isolation from it.

39. Principle 19 stipulates that the States shall provide prior and timely notification and relevant information to potentially affected States on activities that may have a significant adverse trans-boundary environment effect and shall consult with those States at an early stage and in good faith.

40. The Report has emphasized that the members of alert and informed community who are fully aware of the nature of hazards and its impact on their health can help in protecting and saving the natural resources. It has referred to the law enacted in USA in the wake of Bhopal Gas Tragedy, namely, Emergency Planning and Community Right to Act, 1986, which requires preparation of emergency response plans by the companies with involvement of local community. It is also noticed that though Bhopal Gas Tragedy took place in our country, no such legislation has been enacted so far. Further HPC has given example of decision taken by Andhra Pradesh Pollution Control Board which decided that all Industrial factories shall put up two sign boards 6x4 ft. each at publically visible place at the main gate; the first providing information regarding the facility specific consent for establishment and consent for

operating (CFO) conditions and the second providing information of release of pollutants" air emissions, water discharges and solid waste. It has been recommended that public participation should be secured in the management of Environment Pollution and Hazardous Waste to maximum possible extent. Suggestions given in these regards are these :

(i) Selected local residents should be appointed as wardens for environmental surveillance, particularly to take note of illegal dumping of hazardous wastes.

(ii) Access to public records with the environment protection authorities should be freely allowed to the public, as the right to a healthy environment has been defined as part of the Right to Life under Article 21 of the Constitution.

(iii) Relevant important information should be displayed on notice boards and newspapers and communicated through radio, television and the Internet. The HPC would like to see all industries, involved in hazardous chemicals and generating hazardous wastes display on-line date outside the factory gate, on quantity and nature of hazardous chemicals being used in the plant, as well as water and air emissions and solid wastes generated within the factory premises. If such date is not made available, the unit should be asked to show cause or even be asked to close down.

(iv) Informers and "whistle-blowers" within industry who provide information, should be protected and strict confidentiality about them maintained.

(v) Third-party audit of hazardous wastes, where the audit team includes members of the community, should be made a routine practice."

41. The suggestion is that an extensive awareness generation campaign should be taken by regulatory agencies. The HPC has prepared a list of Themes and short T.V. Programmes on hazardous wastes. All these aspects require a serious consideration by the concerned authorities.

42. The legal position has already been noticed. Clearly, the Right to Information and Community Participation necessary for protection of Environment and Human Health is an ineliniable part of Article 21 and is governed by the accepted environment principles. The Government and the authorities have to motivate the public participation by formulating the necessary programmes.

43. Another aspect which deserves to be noticed is about the effect of ship breaking activity covered TOR No.14. We are not suggesting discontinuing of ship breaking activity but it deserves to be strictly and properly regulated. When the ship arrives at a port for breaking, the concerned authorities have to be vigilant about the hazardous waste which may be generated if appropriate timely action by various agencies, in particular, Maritime Board and the SPCB are not taken. The major ship breaking activity in India is at Alang in State of Gujarat and, therefore, Gujarat Maritime Board and Gujarat SPCB have to be alive to the consequences of the appropriate steps to be taken before the breaking activities start. According to the recommendation of HPC, the Inter-Ministerial Committee comprising Ministry of Surface Transport, Ministry of Steel, Ministry of Labour and Ministry of Environment should be constituted with the involvement of Labour and Environment organizations and representatives of the ship breaking Industries.

44. The ship breaking operation referred to above cannot be permitted to be continued without strictly adhering to all precautionary principles, CPCB guidelines and taking the requisite safeguards which have been dealt extensively in the report of precautionary principles, CPCB guidelines and taking the requisite safeguards which have been dealt with extensively in the report of HPC which include the aspect of the working conditions of the workmen.

❑❑❑

55. In the above background, in addition to directions as aforenoticed, for the present, we issue the following further directions:

(2) Ship Breaking:-

We accept the following recommendations of HPC:

1. Before a ship arrives at port, it should have proper consent from the concerned authority or the State Maritime Board, stating that it does not contain any hazardous waste or radioactive substances. AERE should be consulted in the matter in appropriate cases.
2. The ship should be properly decontaminated by the ship owner prior to the breaking. This should be ensured by the SPCBs.

3. Waste generated by the ship breaking process should be classified into hazardous and non-hazardous categories, and their quantify should be made known to the concerned authority or the State Maritime Board.

4. Disposal of waste material, viz. Oil, cotton, dead cargo of inorganic material like hydrated/solidified elements, thermocol pieces, glass wool, rubber, broken tiles, etc. should be done in a proper manner, utilising technologies that meet the criteria of an effective destruction efficiently of 99.9 per cent, with no generation of persistent organic pollutants, and complete containment of all gaseous, liquid and solid residues for analysis and, if needed, reprocessing. Such disposed of material should be kept at a specified placed earmarked for this purpose. Special care must be taken in the handling of asbestos wastes, and total quantities of such waste should be made known to the concerned authorities. The Gujarat Pollution Control Board should authorise appropriate final disposal of asbestos waste.

5. The ship breaking industries should be given authorisation under Rule 5 of the H.W. Rules, 2003, only if they have provisions for disposal of the waste in environmentally sound manner. All authorizations should be renewed only if an industry has facilities for disposal of waste in environmentally sound manner.

6. The State Maritime Board should insist that all quantities of waste oil, sludge and other similar mineral oils and paints chips are carefully removed from the ship and taken immediately to areas outside the beach, for safe disposal.

7. There should be immediatc ban of burning of any material whether hazardous or non hazardous on the beach.

8. The State Pollution Control Board (of Gujarat and other coastal States where this ship breaking activity is done) be directed to close all units which are not authorized under the HW Rules.

9. That the plots where no activities are being currently conducted should not be allowed to commence any fresh ship breaking activity unless they have necessary authorization.

10. The Gujarat PCBs should ensure continuous monitoring of ambient air and noise level as per the standards fixed. The Gujarat PCBs be further directed to install proper equipment and infrastructure for analysis to enable it to conduct first level inspection of hazardous material, radio-

active substances (wherever applicable). AER shall be consulted in such cases.

11. The Gujarat SPCB will ensure compliance of the new Gujarat Maritime Board (Prevention of Fire & Accidents for Safety & Welfare of Workers and Protection of Environment during Ship breaking Activities) Regulations, 2000, by Gujarat Maritime Board and should submit a compliance report to the Court within one year of the coming into force of the said regulations.

12. The Notification issued by GMB in 2001 on Gas Free for Hot Work, should be made mandatory and no ship should be given a beaching permission unless this certificates is shown. Any explosion irrespective of the possession of certification should be dealt sternly and the license of the plot holder should be cancelled and Explosives inspector should be prosecuted accordingly for giving false certificate.

13. A complete inventory of hazardous waste on board of ship should be made mandatory for the ship owner. And not breaking permission should be granted without such an inventory. This inventory should also be submitted by the GMB to concerned SPCBs to ensure safe disposal of hazardous and toxics waste.

14. Gujarat Maritime Board and Gujarat SPCB officers should visit sites at regular intervals so that the plot owner know that these institutions are serious about improvement in operational standards. An Inter-Ministerial Committee comprising Ministry of Surface Transport, Ministry of Steel, Ministry of Labour and Ministry of Environment should be constituted with the involvement of labour and environment organizations and representatives of the ship breaking industry.

15. The SPCBs along with the State Maritime Board should prepare land fill sites and incinerators as per the CPCB guidelines and only after prior approval of the CPCB. This action should be taken in a time bound manner. The maximum time allowed should be one year.

16. At the international level, India should participate in international meetings on ship breaking at the level of the International Maritime Organization and the Basel Convention's Technical Working Group with a clear mandate for the decontamination of ships of their hazardous substances such as asbestos, waste oil, gas and PCBs prior to exports to India for breaking. Participation should include from Central and State level.

17. The continuation or expansion of the Alang ship breaking operations should be permitted subject to compliance with the above recommendations by the plot holders.

18. That the above conditions also apply to other ship-breaking activities in other coastal states."

❑❑❑

56. With the aforesaid directions the matters are adjourned.

(Y.K. Sabharwal J)

New Delhi

October 14, 2003

(B.N. Agrawal J)

[THE SUPREME COURT OF INDIA GRANTED PERMISSION TO DISMANTLE 'THE BLUE LADY' BY THIS JUDGMENT. FULL TEXT OF THE JUDGMENT IS REPRODUCED HERE]

THE SUPREME COURT OF INDIA

I.A. No. 34 of 2006

IN

Writ Petition (civil) 657 of 1995

Research Foundation for Science Technology and Natural Resource Policy .....PETITIONER

Versus

Union of India and Others .....RESPONDENT

DATE OF JUDGMENT: 11/09/2007

BENCH: Dr. Arijit Pasayat& S. H. Kapadia

JUDGMENT

S.H. Kapadia, J.

1. A short question which arises for determination in this IA is whether this Court should grant permission for dismantling of the ship "Blue Lady" at Alang, Gujarat.

2. The "Blue Lady" ex SS Norway was a passenger liner built at Chantier De Altantic, St. Nazaire, France in 1961. It was a steam turbine driven vessel with a power and rating of 30,000 KW and 40,760 HP respectively. Now the vessel is registered as a Barge under the flag of Bahamas vide official number 710763. The vessel is very luxurious in its kind and many dignitaries like President of America, Queen of England have travelled during its golden period. The said ship was beached on 15/16.8.2006 off the Alang coast. The said ship was the passenger ship. It was constructed in 1952. It originated from France. Its last origin was from Norway. The ship is about 291 mt. long. It is 34 mt. wide. It has the capacity of 45886 MT. It has 16 floors. It has 1400 rooms for passengers accommodation. It has restaurant, cinema, health club and free shopping complex.

3. Alang is located on the west coast of Gujarat. It is the largest ship recycling yard in the world. It is one of the choicest ship-scrapping

destination for the ship owners around the world. There are 183 plots in all to carry out the ship recycling activities. Till today Alang has provided approximately 23 million tonnes of steel in the last 10 years. On 17.2.2006 when the above writ petition came up for hearing before this Court, we found the controversy concerning ship-breaking a recurring controversy. Therefore, this Court decided to lay down norms concerning infrastructure, capacity of Alang to handle large volume of ship-breaking activity, safeguards to be provided to the workers who were likely to face health- hazard on account of the incidence of ship-breaking activity, the environmental impact assessment, regulation of the said activity and strict regulation of the said activity. Accordingly, this Court constituted a Committee of Technical Experts to submit a report on the aforestated aspects.

4. We quote hereinbelow the said order dated 17.2.2006:

> "It is brought to our notice that the ship Clemenceau has been directed to be taken back to France. Therefore, immediate controversy relating to Clemenceau ship seems to be over. But the problem is a recurring one. First and foremost requirement as of today is to find out the infrastructural stability and adequacy of the ship breaking yard at Alang. It has to be found out whether the same are operational/operating in a way that environmental hazards and pollution are avoided and/or equipped to meet the requirements in that regard. For that purpose, it is necessary to constitute a Committee of technical experts who can, after obtaining views and inviting suggestions from those who would like to give them to find out whether the infrastructure as existing at Alang presently is adequate. If according to the Committee, it is not adequate it shall indicate the deficiencies, and shall also suggest remedial measures to upgrade the infrastructural facilities. For this purpose, Union of India shall, as early as practicable, constitute a Committee of technical experts, some of them having Navy background, preferably retired officers. The Committee shall submit its report to this Court within eight weeks. The expenses of the Committee shall be met by the Ministry of Environment and Forests. Since at various points of time various guidelines have been indicated, it would be appropriate if they are properly codified to be followed scrupulously by all concerned including the Government authorities."

5. In continuation of the said order dated 17.2.2006 a further order was passed by this Court on 12.3.2007 calling for a further report by TEC in which this Court directed inclusion of Gujarat Maritime Board (GMB) and Gujarat Pollution Control Board (GPCB) to assist this Court on three aspects, namely, pre-conditions to be satisfied by the recycler for dismantling and reusability of 80% of the asbestos. This Court also sought assistance of various authorities, including the petitioner herein, on steps to be taken to control the environmental impact of asbestos dust likely to be generated in the process of dismantling. We quote hereinbelow the said order in extenso:

> "Having heard learned counsel for the parties, we are of the view that a further report by the T.E.C. is required to indicate as to whether conditions stipulated have been complied with before any action can be taken on the dismantling plan. Let the applicant in I.A. No.34 place materials before T.E.C. as to how and in what manner compliance has been done. While deciding the acceptability of the stand of the applicant, the T.E.C. shall involve the Gujarat Maritime Board and the Gujarat Pollution Control Board and take note of their views. In the report apart from examining the general compliance of the conditions, specific focus has to be drawn on three particular aspects, namely,
>
> (a) whether pre-conditions for dismantling have been complied with; (b) whether 80% of the asbestos is reusable as is contended by the applicant; (c) what steps have been taken to control the environmental impact of asbestos dust generated in the process of dismantling. The T.E.C. shall also suggest as to which agency shall oversee and monitor the dismantling in case it recommends acceptance of the dismantling plan. The report shall be submitted within six weeks. The other aspects relating to the reversibility or impermissibility of the beaching, manner of dealing with hazardous from asbestos and other hazardous material shall be considered after the receipt of the report from the T.E.C. The T.E.C. which was constituted pursuant to the order of this court having submitted its report is stated to have become functus officio shall examine the matter as directed."

6. Ultimately, the TEC submitted its report on the aforestated aspects on 10.5.2007. That report has been accepted by this Court vide order

dated 6.9.2007 in writ petition no. 657/95 etc.. We accepted that report mainly because it is all pervasive. It contains opinions of experts including retired navel officers. It indicates State-of-the-Art mechanism to regulate removal of asbestos. The report clarifies that "beaching" is an irreversible process. TEC has also examined the recycling plan and the dismantling plan submitted by the recycler. Apart from the GMB and GPCB, various other authorities like Gujarat Enviro Protection & Infrastructure Ltd. (GEPIL) have also contributed their knowledge and expertise in the preparation of the report dated 10.5.2007. There was also an apprehension rightly expressed by the petitioner regarding radio active material on board the vessel "Blue Lady". Therefore, an immediate inspection of the said vessel beached at Alang since 16.8.2006 was undertaken by Atomic Energy Regulatory Board (AERB) and by GMB. The apprehension expressed by the petitioner was right. However, as the matter stands today, AERB and GMB have certified that the said vessel Blue Lady beached in Alang no more contains any radio active material on board the ship.

7. By the said report dated 10.5.2007, which has been accepted by us vide order dated 6.9.2007, TEC has also recommended grant of permission for dismantling of the ship "Blue Lady" at Alang (Gujarat) in accordance with the recycling plan submitted by M/s Priya Blue Industries Pvt. Ltd. (recycler). Under the said report, TEC has stated that regular monitoring of the ship-breaking operations of Blue Lady shall be undertaken by the competent authority mentioned in the report so as to ensure strict compliance with the guidelines given by TEC in respect of safety and health of the workmen and environment. At this stage, we may mention that breaking of the vessel Blue Lady will provide to this country 41000 MT of steel and it would give employment to 700 workmen.

8. In his Keynote Address, on 'Global Constitutionalism', reported in Stanford Law Review vol. 59 at p. 1155, Lord Goldsmith, Her Majesty's Attorney General (UK), stated that British Constitution though unwritten is based on three principles, namely, rule of law, commitment to fundamental freedoms and principle of proportionality. European Convention on Human Rights ("ECHR") also refers to the concept of balance.

9. In the case of Research Foundation for Science Technology National Resource Policy v. Union of India and Anr. (2005) 10 SCC 510 a Division

Bench of this Court has held that "precautionary principle" is a part of the concept of sustainable development. We quote hereinbelow paragraphs 16 and 43 of the said judgment, which are as follows:

"16. The legal position regarding applicability of the precautionary principle and polluter-pays principle which are part of the concept of sustainable development in our country is now well settled. In Vellore Citizens' Welfare Forum v. Union of India (1996) 5 SCC 647 a three-Judge Bench of this Court, after referring to the principles evolved in various international conferences and to the concept of "sustainable development", inter alia, held that the precautionary principle and polluter-pays principle have now emerged and govern the law in our country, as is clear from Articles 47, 48-A and 51-A (g) of our Constitution and that, in fact, in the various environmental statutes including the Environment (Protection) Act, 1986, these concepts are already implied. These principles have been held to have become part of our law. Further, it was observed in Vellore Citizens' Welfare Forum case that these principles are accepted as part of the customary international law and hence there should be no difficulty in accepting them as part of our domestic law. Reference may also be made to the decision in the case of A.P. Pollution Control Board v. Prof. M.V. Nayudu (1999) 2 SCC 718 where, after referring to the principles noticed in Vellore Citizens' Welfare Forum case the same have been explained in more detail with a view to enable the courts and the tribunals or environmental authorities to properly apply the said principles in the matters which come before them. In this decision, it has also been observed that the principle of good governance is an accepted principle of international and domestic laws. It comprises of the rule of law, effective State institutions, transparency and accountability and public affairs, respect for human rights and the meaningful participation of citizens in the political process of their countries and in the decisions affecting their lives. Reference has also been made to Article 7 of the draft approved by the Working Group of the International Law Commission in 1996 on "Prevention of Transboundary Damage from Hazardous Activities" to include the need for the State to take necessary "legislative, administrative and other actions" to implement the duty of prevention of environmental harm. Environmental concerns have been placed on the same pedestal as human rights concerns, both being traced to Article 21 of the Constitution. It is the duty of this Court to render justice by taking all aspects into consideration. It has also been observed that with a view to ensure that there is neither danger to the environment nor to the ecology and, at the same time, ensuring sustainable development, the court can refer scientific and technical aspects for an investigation and opinion to expert bodies. The provisions of a covenant which elucidate and go to effectuate the fundamental rights guaranteed by our Constitution, can be relied upon by courts as facets of those fundamental rights and hence enforceable as such (see People's Union for Civil Liberties v. Union of India (1997) 3 SCC 433. The Basel Convention, it cannot be doubted, effectuates the fundamental rights guaranteed under Article 21. The right to information and community participation for protection of environment and human health is also a right which flows from Article 21. The Government and authorities have, thus to motivate the public participation. These well-enshrined principles have been kept in view by us while examining and determining various aspects and facets of the problems in issue and the permissible remedies.

x x x

43. Another aspect which deserves to be noticed is about the effect of ship-breaking activity covered by TOR (14). We are not suggesting discontinuing of ship- breaking activity but it deserves to be strictly and properly regulated. When the ship arrives at a port for breaking, the authorities concerned have to be vigilant about the hazardous waste which may be generated if appropriate timely action by various agencies, in particular, the Maritime Board and SPCB are not taken. The major ship-breaking activity in India is at Alang in the State of Gujarat and, therefore, the Gujarat Maritime Board and Gujarat SPCB have to be alive to the consequences of the appropriate steps to be taken before the breaking activities start. According to the recommendations of HPC, the Inter-Ministerial Committee comprising Ministry of Surface Transport, Ministry of Steel, Ministry of Labour and Ministry of Environment should be constituted with the involvement of labour and environment organisations and representatives of the ship-breaking industries.

(emphasis supplied)

10. The concept of "balance" under the principle of proportionality applicable in the case of sustainable development is lucidly explained by Pasayat, J. in the judgment of this Court in the case of T.N. Godavarman Thirumalpad v. Union of India and Ors. reported in (2002) 10 SCC 606 vide para 35 which reads as under:

> "35. It cannot be disputed that no development is possible without some adverse effect on the ecology and environment, and the projects of public utility cannot be abandoned and it is necessary to adjust the interest of the people as well as the necessity to maintain the environment. A balance has to be struck between the two interests. Where the commercial venture or enterprise would bring in results which are far more useful for the people, difficulty of a small number of people has to be bypassed. The comparative hardships have to be balanced and the convenience and benefit to a larger section of the people has to get primacy over comparatively lesser hardship."

The above paragraphs indicate that while applying the concept of "sustainable development" one has to keep in mind the "principle of proportionality" based on the concept of balance. It is an exercise in which we have to balance the priorities of development on one hand and environmental protection on the other hand.

11. India after globalization is an emergent economy along with Brazil, Russia and China. India has economic growth of above 9%. However, that growth is lop-sided. A large section of the population lives below poverty line. India has largest number of youth in the world. Unemployment is endemic. Article 21/14 is the heart of the Chapter of fundamental rights. Equality of opportunity is the basic theme of Article 14. In an emergent economy, the principle of proportionality based on the concept of balance is important. It provides level playing field to different stakeholders. Ship breaking is an industry. When we apply the principle of sustainable development, we need to keep in mind the concept of development on one hand and the concepts like generation of revenue, employment and public interest on the other hand. This is where the principle of proportionality comes in. Even in the case of Blue Lady, the figures indicate that 700 workers would be employed in ship breaking. Further, 41000 MT of steel would be made available. To that extent, there will be less pressure on mining activity elsewhere. Even in

the judgment, referred to above, vide para 43, it has been observed that this Court is not in favour of discontinuance of ship-breaking activity. However, this Court has held that the said activity needs to be strictly and properly regulated. This concept of balancing is given importance by Dr. Amartya Sen in his book "Development as Freedom". Today ship-breaking provides resources not only in terms of steel but also in terms of employment, skill and capability. Competition exists in the said business of ship-breaking amongst Bangladesh, Pakistan and India. In our view, if "capability" is a resource with our skilled workers it needs to be protected by strict implementation of Health Hazard Preventive Measures suggested in the report of TEC and implementation of Recycling Plans, generation of pollutants like asbestos to the extent of 20% can be almost eliminated. As stated, 85% of asbestos is in form of ACM in panels which is reusable. Therefore, the report provides State-of-the-Art mechanism which is the key element of "sustainable development".

12. One of the main objections raised on behalf of the petitioner was regarding non-quantification of two contaminants, namely, ACM and PCB (rubber). At this stage, we may clarify that ACM exists as material of construction in various vessel components like partitions, walls, ceilings etc. which are an integral part of the vessel structure. In the present case, the vessel does not contain single kilogram of asbestos and/ or ACM as cargo. However, there is presence of ACM as "material of construction" in various vessel components like partitions, walls, ceiling etc.. Major quantity of ACM (85%) is in the partitions and ceilings of rooms and galleries. These ACMs are in the panels. TEC, in its report, stated that recyclable material alone can be sold, therefore, PCB cannot be sold. The report further indicates that the quantity of PCB in the present case has to be dumped in land-fills. It is important to note that there are only two alternatives, namely, incineration or dumping PCB in land-fills. In both the cases, there is likelihood of pollution. As regards asbestos is concerned, we find that 85% is insulation and panels. This is where the dismantling plan has to be applied. It is this plan which takes care of the panels and insulation containing asbestos. Under section 3.3.2, the recycler was required to submit a dismantling plan containing requirements to be complied with. We quote hereinbelow section 3.3.2 of the report of the Committee of Technical Experts on Ship Breaking Activities dated 30.8.2006:

"**3.3.2. Ship Dismantling Plan:**

Before starting the recycling process, the recycler should submit a Dismantling Plan to the authorities, which should include:

(a) Details about the ship, and in particular, a fair assessment of hazardous wastes/hazardous materials.

(b) Ship breaking schedules with sequence of work.

(c) Operational work procedures.

(d) Availability of material handling equipment and PPEs.

(e) Plan for removal of oil and cleaning of tanks.

(f) Hazardous waste handling and disposal plan.

(g) 'Gas-free and fit for hot work' certificate issued by the Department of Explosives, or any competent agency authorized by the Department of Explosives.

(h) Identification and marking of all non-breathable spaces by the Recycler.

(i) Identification and marking of all places containing/likely to contain hazardous substances/hazardous wastes.

(j) Confirmation to the effect that ballast water has been exchanged in the high seas. The tasks should address all the three phases of recycling, i.e.

(i) Preparation phase.

(ii) Dismantling phase.

(iii) Waste stream management

(k) Asbestos being a major area of concern, the scheme for removing asbestos, and asbestos containing materials (ACMs) on board, and on shore, should be specifically provided. The plan should include arrangements for handling, treatment and disposal. Locations having asbestos/ACMs should be marked before commencing dismantling operations.

(l) Systems and procedures to be followed to document and keep track of all hazardous waste generated during recycling, as well as hazardous substances found onboard the ship, and their transport to the disposal facility or registered recycling facility should be provided."

13. The report dated 10.5.2007 of TEC states that the Dismantling Plan submitted by recycler in the case of Blue Lady complies with section 3.3.2. As stated above, the "precautionary principle" is embedded in the doctrine of sustainable development. In the present case, one of the main apprehensions, justifiable, concerns removal of ACM and PCB from engine room, vent room and insulated pipelines. According to the removal plan, all major quantity of ACM (85%) is in form of wall partitions, ceiling and roofing in rooms and gallery. It is reusable. Therefore, the panels, partitions, ceilings etc. have to be removed in such a way that the ACMs are not damaged. The removal plan submitted by the recycler has been approved by the TEC. Similarly, air monitoring has to be conducted for the air-borne ACM, if any. For that purpose the Committee has recommended appropriate respiratory protection to be provided to the workmen. For each category of work to be done in different areas of the vessel, gears have been provided to the workmen in the form of whole body coveralls, gloves, safety shoes, helmet, safety goggles etc. Similarly, as regards waste generation, the TEC report suggests by way of protection air monitoring respiratory protection to employees, leak tests, negative pressure checks etc. Similarly, storage of contaminated wastes in the land-fills has also been incorporated in the recommendations of the TEC. Therefore, in our view, in the light of the above conditions to be fulfilled by the recycler, the principle of sustainable development based on the concept of "balance" stands satisfied.

14. We may mention one important aspect. Asbestos in the panel exists even in false ceiling constructed in commercial establishments. It is only when those panels are broken that asbestos as a hazardous substance emerges. In the present case, 85% of the asbestos is in the panels and insulation that quantity is reusable. As far as dismantling is concerned, the plan complies with section 3.3.2. However, it is likely that in some cases asbestos as a substance may emerge and, therefore, the report of TEC has taken care to look into and approve the Recycling Management Plan.

15. In our view, the report of TEC is foolproof. It has taken into account international standards to regulate ship-breaking activity. The quantity of PCB has been determined by Gujarat Enviro Protection & Infrastructure Ltd. ("GEPIL"). There is NOC given by GMB as also by GPCB in the matter of ship- breaking of the ship "Blue Lady". The report dated 10.5.2007 has evolved State-of-the-Art mechanism to regulate removal of asbestos. Recycling is a key element of sustainable development. The

Committee has examined each and every aspect concerning recycling and dismantling of the ship "Blue Lady". Lastly, we may point out that there is no dispute that on 15/16.8.2006 the vessel beached off Alang coast. It is not in dispute that the process of beaching is irreversible. Taking into account the contours of TEC report dated 10.5.2007 and the opinion of TEC that the recycler M/s Priya Blue Industries Pvt. Ltd. has complied with the norms regarding dismantling and recycling, we accept the report of the TEC dated 10.5.2007 and we accordingly grant permission to the said recycler to dismantle the said ship "Blue Lady" as recommended by TEC (see: para 12 of the TEC report dated 10.5.2007).

15. Accordingly the I.A. stands disposed of.

(Dr.Arjit Pasayat J)

(S. H. Kapadia J)

New Delhi;
September 11, 2007

[This was the final judgment by which the Supreme Court of India had finally decided the Writ Petition. The Supreme Court directed that the Government of India should put a total ban on all hazardous wastes which have been identified by the BASEL Convention and its Protocols over the years and/or where imports into the country have been restricted by the municipal laws of India. The Court re-emphasized that the restrictions contained in the BASEL Convention have to be strictly followed by all the concerned players before a vessel is allowed to enter Indian territorial waters and beach at any of the beaching facilities in any part of the Indian coast-line. In case of breach of the conditions, the authorities shall impose the penalties contemplated under the municipal laws of India. For full text see: https://indiankanoon.org/doc/58220473/]

IN THE SUPREME COURT OF INDIA
CIVIL ORIGINAL JURISDICTION
WRIT PETITION (C) No.657 of 1995

RESEARCH FOUNDATION FOR SCIENCE, TECHNOLOGY AND NATURAL RESOURCE POLICY ... PETITIONER

VS.

UNION OF INDIA & ORS. ...RESPONDENTS

EXCERPTS OF THE JUDGMENT DATED 6th JULY, 2012.

ALTAMAS KABIR, J.

1. This writ petition has been filed by the Research Foundation for Science Technology and Natural Resource Policy, through its Director, Ms. Vandana Shiva, for the following reliefs :

   "1. direct the Union of India banning all imports of all hazardous/toxic wastes;

   2. direct amendment of rules in conformity with the BASEL Convention and Article 21, 47 and 48A of the Constitution as interpreted by this Court;

   3. declare that without adequate protection to the workers and public and without any provision of sound environment management

of disposal of hazardous/toxic wastes, the Hazardous Wastes (Management & Handling) Rules, 1989 are violative of Fundamental Rights and, therefore, unconstitutional;"

On 29th October, 1995, this Court directed notice to issue on the writ petition and also on the application for stay.

2. The basic grievance of the Writ Petitioner was with regard to the import of toxic wastes from industrialized countries to India, despite such wastes being hazardous to the environment and life of the people of this country. The Writ Petitioner sought to challenge the decision of the Ministry of Environment and Forests permitting import of toxic wastes in India under the cover of recycling, which, according to the Petitioner, made India a dumping ground for toxic wastes. It was alleged that these decisions were contrary to the provisions of Articles 14 and 21 of the Constitution and also Article 47, which enjoins a duty on the State to raise the standards of living and to improve public health. In the writ petition it was also contended that Article 48A provides that the State shall endeavour to protect and improve the environment and to safeguard the forests and wildlife of the country.

❐❐❐

18. At the very beginning of this judgment we have set out the reliefs prayed for in the writ petition, which, inter alia, include a prayer for a direction upon the Union of India to ban imports of all hazardous/toxic wastes and for a further direction to amend the rules in conformity with the BASEL Convention and Articles 21, 47 and 48A of the Constitution. Apart from the above, a declaration has also been sought that without adequate protection of the workers and the public and without any provision of sound environment management of disposal of hazardous/toxic wastes, the Hazardous Wastes (Management & Handling) Rules, 1989, are violative of the Fundamental Rights guaranteed under the Constitution and, therefore, unconstitutional.

19. Since the proceedings became a continuing mandamus, this Court from time to time took up several issues emanating from the first prayer in the writ petition to ban imports of all hazardous/toxic wastes. However, in the process, one of the Conventions, namely, the impact of the MARPOL Convention, though referred to, was not decided and left for decision at the final hearing. Accordingly, that aspect of the matter has to be decided also in these proceedings.

20. In one of the earlier orders passed on 5th May, 1997, two Hon'ble Judges had occasion to deal with the enormous generation of hazardous wastes in the country each day and Their Lordships were of the opinion that the said fact alone indicated sufficiently the magnitude of the problem and the promptitude with which it was needed to be tackled before the damage became irreversible. Their Lordships observed that prompt action was required to be taken, not only by the Central Government, but also by the State Governments and the Central and the State Pollution Control Boards. Accordingly, notice was given to all the State Governments and the State Control Boards to file their replies, and directions were also given that with effect from that date no authorization/ permission would be given by any authority for the import of wastes which had already been banned by the Central Government or by any order made by any Court or any other authority. In addition, it was also directed that with effect from the date of the order, no import would be made or permitted by any authority or any person of any hazardous waste, which was already banned under the Basel Convention or was to be banned subsequently, with effect from the date specified therein. Notice was also issued to the State Governments to show cause as to why an order should not be made directing closure of the units utilizing the hazardous wastes where provision had already been made for requisite safe disposal sites. In addition, the State Governments were also directed to show cause as to why immediate orders should not be made for the closure of all unauthorized hazardous waste handling units.

❑❑❑

30. India is a signatory, both to the BASEL Convention as also the MARPOL Convention, and is, therefore, under an obligation to ensure that the same are duly implemented in relation to import of hazardous wastes into the country. As we have noticed earlier, the BASEL Convention prohibited the import of certain hazardous substances on which there was a total ban. However, some of the other pollutants, which have been identified, are yet to be notified and, on the other hand, in order to prevent pollution of the seas, under the MARPOL Convention the signatory countries are under an obligation to accept the discharge of oil wastes from ships. What is, therefore, important is for the concerned authorities to ensure that such waste oil is not allowed to contaminate the surrounding areas

and also, if suitable, for the purposes of recycling, to allow recycling of the same under strict supervision with entrusted units and, thereafter, to oversee its distribution for reuse.

31. As far as the first two prayers in the writ petition are concerned, the same have already been taken care of by the orders dated 13th October, 1997 and 14th October, 2003. By the first of the two orders, this Court appointed the High-Powered Committee with Prof. M.G.K. Menon as its Chairman and 14 issues were referred to the said Committee. After the said Committee submitted its Report, another Committee under the Chairmanship of Mr. A.C. Wadhawan was appointed to enquire into the disappearance of hazardous wastes from various ports and container depots, and the question relating to the working conditions of the workmen who handle such wastes. After the Wadhawan Committee submitted its Report, various directions were given with regard to the handling of such hazardous wastes. Furthermore, the contamination risks involved in ship breaking also came into focus in the light of the provisions of the Hazardous Wastes Rules, 1989, and directions were given as to how ships, which were carrying wastes, were to be dealt with before entering into Indian waters, which included the prohibition on the exporting country to export such oil or substance without the concurrence and clearance from the importing country. During the course of hearing, an issue was raised by Mr. Sanjay Parikh, learned counsel appearing for the petitioner, that some conditions may be laid down in relation to vessels containing hazardous wastes entering Indian waters without proper compliance with the provisions of the BASEL and the MARPOL Conventions. However, since the question of ship breaking and distribution of hazardous wastes are being considered separately in the contempt proceedings, in these proceedings we expect and reiterate that the directions contained in the BASEL Convention have to be strictly followed by all the concerned players, before a vessel is allowed to enter Indian territorial waters and beach at any of the beaching facilities in any part of the Indian coast-line. In case of breach of the conditions, the authorities shall impose the penalties contemplated under the municipal laws of India.

32. The directions contained in the second order is based on the polluter pays principle, which is duly recognized as one of the accepted principles for dealing with violation of the BASEL Convention and the H.W.M.H. Rules, 1989, and the same will be applicable whenever

such violations occur. However, till such time as a particular product is identified as being hazardous, no ban can be imposed on its import on the ground that it was hazardous. Such import will, however, be subject to all other statutory conditions and restrictions, as may be prevailing on the date of import. Accordingly, the general prayer made in the writ petition that the Government of India should put a total ban on all hazardous wastes, can be applied in respect of such hazardous wastes as have been identified by the BASEL Convention and its Protocols over the years and/or where import into the country have been restricted by the municipal laws of India. In respect of such banned items, directions have already been given in the order dated 13th October, 1997, to issue a notification to ban the import of such identified hazardous substances. In the event, any other items have since been identified, the Central Government is directed to issue appropriate notifications for banning the import of such hazardous substances as well.

33. The third prayer, that in the event of non-compliance, the provisions of the Hazardous Wastes (Management & Handling) Rules, 1989, should be declared as unconstitutional, cannot be granted, since the same are in aid and not in derogation of the provisions of Articles 21, 39(e), 47 and 48A of the Constitution. In fact, as mentioned hereinabove, even at the interim stage, directions were given for compliance with the said Rules, particularly in the matter of destruction of the waste oil contained in 170 containers by incineration at the cost of the importer.

34. The writ petition has been entertained and has also been treated by all concerned not as any kind of adversarial litigation, but litigation to protect the environment from contamination on account of attempts made to dump hazardous wastes in the country, which would ultimately result in the destruction, not only of the environment, but also the ecology as well and, in particular, the fragile marine bio-diversity along the Indian Coast- line. The petitioner Foundation has played a very significant role in bringing into focus some very serious questions involving the introduction of hazardous substances into the country, which needed the Courts' attention to be drawn having regard to the BASEL Convention, aimed and protecting marine biology and countries having coast-lines alongside seas and oceans.

35. The writ petition is, therefore, disposed of by reasserting the interim directions given with regard to the handling of hazardous wastes and

ship breaking in the various orders passed in the writ petition from time to time and, in particular, the orders dated 13th October, 1997 and 14th October, 2003. The Central Government is also directed to ban import of all hazardous/toxic wastes which had been identified and declared to be so under the BASEL Convention and its different protocols. The Central Government is also directed to bring the Hazardous Wastes (Management & Handling) Rules, 1989, in line with the BASEL Convention and Articles 21, 47 and 48A of the Constitution. The further declaration sought for that without adequate protection to the workers and public, the aforesaid Rules are violative of the Fundamental Rights of the citizens and are, therefore, unconstitutional, is, however, rejected in view of what has been discussed hereinabove.

36. In the peculiar facts of the case, there will be no order as to costs.

(Altamas Kabir J)
(J. Chelameswar J)

New Delhi
Dated: 6th July, 2012.